The Life of Jane Dormer, Duchess of Feria

Quarterly Series

SIXTY-SECOND VOLUME

THE LIFE OF THE DUCHESS OF FERIA

PRINTED AT ST. ANNE'S PRESS
PERCY STREET LONDON W

THE LIFE OF JANE DORMER
DUCHESS OF FERIA

BY

HENRY CLIFFORD

*Transcribed from the Ancient Manuscript in the possession
of the Lord Dormer*

BY THE LATE

CANON E. E. ESTCOURT

AND EDITED BY THE

REV. JOSEPH STEVENSON

OF THE SOCIETY OF JESUS

LONDON
BURNS AND OATES
LIMITED
GRANVILLE MANSIONS W
1887

PREFACE.

THE following pages contain an interesting
sketch of the life of Jane Dormer, Duchess of
Feria, extending from the time of her birth
during the reign of king Henry the Eighth to
that of her death in the reign of James the
First. It contains many interesting details
respecting the personal character and social
condition of various individuals with whom it
is instructive to become thus familiarly acquainted. Its author commands at once our attention and our confidence by reminding us of his
own personal knowledge of most of the incidents which he has here recorded. He was
an inmate of the family of the Duchess; he
had resided for many years in her household;
he possessed her confidence, he witnessed her
death and assisted at her funeral. We feel

that we may trust his statements without hesitation. He writes with a quiet simplicity which recommends what he has here chronicled; and we gladly, accept his story, homely as it is, as more than a compensation for that lack of artistic skill which the reader cannot fail to detect in the structure of the following narrative.

Our chronicle opens with a sketch of the history of the noble family of Dormer, the accuracy of which, in some of its earlier details, may possibly be questioned. But the attention of the reader is speedily arrested by the precious details with which it furnishes him respecting the life, sufferings and death of Father Sebastian Nudigate, who takes his place along with Cardinal Fisher and Sir Thomas More among the noble army of martyrs who died for the faith under Henry the Eighth.[1] Several interesting particulars as to the private character and domestic virtues of Queen Catharine of Aragon next claim our notice. We learn that she rose at midnight to

[1] P. 1).

be present at the Matins of the Religious, after which she heard Mass at five o'clock in the morning. Under her royal attire she wore the habit of St. Francis, "having taken the profession of his Third Order." She fasted on bread and water every Friday and Saturday, and on all the eves of our Blessed Lady, whose Office she read daily. On every Sunday she received the Blessed Sacrament of the Altar. Most part of her morning was spent in the Church at holy Service, and after dinner she read the life of the Saint of the day to her maids. And then she returned to the Church. She was banished from the Court to Kimbolton, where it was said that her days had been shortened by the unwholesome air, while some were of opinion that poison had been administered, "for the lady Anne hated her extremely." [2]

Of Anne Boleyn a few characteristic sketches are preserved. Her life was very different to that of her predecessor, being passed chiefly in masks, plays, dancing and such personal de-

[2] P. 73-78.

lights, "in which she had a special grace." Our author has preserved a story, which he believed to be true, of Anne having attempted to poison Cardinal Fisher; and he states that the agent in the plot "being discovered did confess it and was publicly put to death for it." Several other reports of a kindred nature follow; which, be they true or false, show the estimation in which Anne's morality was generally regarded by her contemporaries.[8]

Edward the Sixth next claims at once our attention and our sympathy. In order that the new doctrine now introduced into England might take the deeper root, we are told that apostate priests and friars from foreign parts, with their wives, were entertained in this kingdom, and sent to be public preachers in the Universities, where they taught heresies. If any pious or learned Catholic gainsaid (as many did) the doctrine of these outlandish apostates, they were persecuted, put to silence, deprived of their livings, imprisoned, or banished. The calm firmness with which this iniquitous

[8] P. 76–85.

attempt was resisted by a considerable number of the English people is well illustrated by the account here given of the conduct of the Princess Mary and the family of the Dormers.

Of the little Prince himself some pleasing reminiscences are here recorded, and they come to us in a form which commands our acceptance. Our Biographer writes as follows. "I have heard them that were about the Prince avouch it, that his inclination was of great towardness to all virtuous parts and princely qualities. He was a marvellous sweet child, of very mild and generous condition. Afterwards when his father died (he being but nine years of age) mischievous and heretical governors, contrary to his father's will, abused his tender age; who ruling to effect their own ends notoriously injured the natural good inclinations of this gentle and noble prince. For, when he was king, in passing by the ruins of goodly monasteries, he demanded what buildings were these; it was answered, that they were religious houses, dissolved and demolished by order of the king his father for abuses. Edward replied; "Could not my father punish the offenders and suffer so goodly buildings to stand, and put in better men that might have governed and inhabited them?" seeming to lament that lamentable course."

From the same authority we learn that the Princess Mary, having gained some influence over the little Edward, order was taken by his tutors that the visits of his half-sister should be very rare, upon the plea that they made him unhappy and melancholy. It was intended also that proceedings should have been taken against Mary's officers and servants for violating the newly made law, she having had public Mass in her chapel; but Edward refused to sanction this prosecution, and strictly commanded that the Princess should have full liberty to follow the dictates of her conscience.[4]

The accession of Elizabeth was a turning-point in the history of Jane Dormer. During the reign of Queen Mary her sister, the Princess Elizabeth had professed herself to be a zealous Catholic, and as such had deliberately practised the duties

[4] P. 61, 62.

required by the Church; but when she found herself safely mounted on the throne of England, she appeared before the world in her true character. The marriage of Jane Dormer to the Count de Feria, Philip's trusted minister, rendered her residence in England no longer possible; and accordingly she bid farewell to the land of her birth, never to return. Her parting interview with Elizabeth and her journey through Flanders and France on her way to her new home in Spain, are here recorded with some minuteness; among the more interesting details of which may be specified the pleasing glimpse which it affords us of the visit which she paid to Mary Stuart, at that time Queen of France and wife of king Francis the Second.

We cannot find space to trace step by step the account here given of the life of the Duchess of Feria during the years which she spent in Spain. In every capacity in which we meet her she appears to advantage; as wife, as mother and as widow; at home and abroad; as mistress of a large household, amidst the temptations of a brilliant court; in her domestic relations with the society with which she mingled, and in her public and private devotions. Just and prudent as well as kindly and generous, she seems to have won the confidence and secured the affections of all with whom she came into contact. While we wish that the narrative of her biographer had been somewhat more diffuse upon certain particulars, we are grateful to him for the details which, but for his loving care would have perished. We treasure the lessons which her example teaches us. Henceforward the name of Jane Dormer, Duchess of Feria, takes its place in our memory as one of that company of good women of which Catholic England has cause to be proud; and we here cordially thank the present noble inheritor of her Name and her Creed, for the privilege of at length becoming acquainted with the virtues of his illustrious ancestress.

And now a few words must be devoted to the insufficient details which have come down to us respecting the author of the following narrative.

The little which we know about the history of Henry Clifford, the biographer of the Duchess of Feria, is derived from the Dormer manuscript.

This narrative, as it stands at the present time, was written in the year 1643, and it was then presented by the author to Charles Dormer, Earl of Carnarvon and Lord Baron of Wing; but it had evidently been drawn up at a much earlier date, while the incidents which are here recorded were fresh in the memory of the narrator. In the Preface to the Life of the Duchess, as we now have it, Clifford tells us that he had derived his information partly from what he himself had seen, known and heard; and partly from the information of trustworthy authorities. From the way in which he mentions an incident which occurred at Oxford when he was a boy there in 1581 or 1582, we may infer that he was born somewhere about the year 1570.[5] He must have been in the service of the Duchess for some time before 1605, for in that year she bestowed upon him an annuity of twenty pounds, as well as the sum of forty pounds due to the Lady Hungerford, lately deceased.[6] He had received information respect-

---

[5] See the present volume, p. 38.

[6] She died 19th December, 1603. See Clifford's letter to Sir Robert Dormer, dated Madrid, 14th December, 1605.

ing the duchess from the Earl of Nottingham, who had seen her when he was ambassador in Spain in 1605.[7] But at this period Clifford had been for some time in the service of the duchess and had secured her confidence, as will appear by the extracts which will presently be given from his correspondence. The narrative was in process of composition, or perhaps of final revision, in 1616.[8] From these indications we may venture to believe that it was begun very shortly after the death of the Duchess of Feria, which occurred on 23rd January, 1613.[9]

During the course of the narrative its author mentions circumstances which shew that he held an official position in the ducal household, and one moreover which brought him into frequent and confidential intercourse with its head. By the duchess he was made acquainted with some conversation of a private nature which had passed between herself and her husband.[10] We have already seen that he was in her service in 1605, at which time he occupied

[7] P. 68.   [8] P. 8.
[9] P. 200.   [10] P. 132.

a situation of trust and authority.[11]   He was in close attendance upon her during her last sickness;[12] he stood by her deathbed in company with two Fathers of the Society of Jesus, four Franciscan Friars, one Dominican and her chaplain;[13] and as she drew her last breath she put into his hands the rosary which she had used, "on which she meditated and had often discoursed."[14]   And as the highest token of their respect for his services, her family entrusted him with the arrangement of her funeral, of the details of which he has left us a full account in the concluding pages of his narrative.

The Manuscript at Grove Park which has furnished the Biography of the Duchess of Feria also contains copies of several letters addressed by Henry Clifford to Sir Robert Dormer (created Baron Dormer of Wing in 1615) the following extracts from which will be read with interest.

---

[11] Pp. 154, 155. See also the extracts from his letters written at this time to Sir Robert Dormer.

[12] Pp. 185, 189.   [13] P. 192.   [14] P. 181.

Madrid, 8th October, 1605.

"I thank God her Grace for her health passeth reasonable well, although troubled often with such infirm and diseaseful accidents as her age is subject unto.

Of the duke of Feria his letters intended for England, as I remember, I certified in my last, and am glad they be received. It argues his honorable disposition that finding by those things he shall receive from you, and from hence, the antiquity and nobility that he hath in his blood from his mother will bind that love and respect which so near affinity requires.

On the 23rd of July there died in Valladolid Sir Thomas Palmer, a Western knight. I think he was of the king's Privy Chamber. His sickness was the small-pox. He died a Catholic and very Christianly."

Madrid, 14 December, 1605.

"If you have not the pedigree ready I pray trouble yourself no further in it, for I shall make a perfect one here, having both the descents by Dormer and Sydney, with their arms and matches,

under Clarencius' hand, as in part you may perceive by this note translated, which I wrote in
Latin for the duke. And when I have finished
the draft as I have devised and her Grace desireth,
against the truth of which no exception shall be
taken, I will send you a copy; wherein you
shall see your house allied with all the great
houses of Christendom. Of the Herald's errors
in the Pedigree you sent I noted in my last,
which were much mistaken.

Her Grace passeth with her health in reasonable sort; and I hope by God His preservation I
shall serve her yet very many years."

Madrid, 22nd March, 1606.

"I thank God her Grace passeth with indifferent
health and beareth her age reasonably well, for on
Twelfth day last she made fully seventy-one years
of age, and yet hath her discretion, judgment and
memory as mature as ever; and you would won-
der to hear how well she discourses in her own
language, with such fit terms and good words as
such English as came hither to visit her marvel
at it; seeing since she left England the language

hath been much altered and refined. But above all her great virtue and admirable example of modest and matron-like carriage give her the honour of all the ladies I know, and without flattery may term her the mirror of her sex and honour of our nation. She hath been widow almost these thirty-eight years [15] and with those remarkable parts of recollection and notable Christianity that all that know her give her much respect and reverence."

Madrid, 17th January, 1609.

"Her Grace (I thank God) enjoys reasonable health, although her many years and the absence of the duque her son, and somewhat the affectionate desire she hath to see your house advanced, deprive her of much contentment; and if she were partaker of these latter she should pass the former with much more ease and comfort.

Yet, sir, if you did know her memory, her discourse, her government, having the management of all her son's estate, the labours that she taketh, rising with the day and presently entering into her oratory, where she remains two

---

[15] But see p. 129 of the present volume.

hours. Then her chaplain comes to say Mass, which ended, if it be a Feast day she goes to church, as every day she does this Holy Week before Easter. If not she disposeth herself to such affairs as are offered. Ever if she have health, in business, for her diet (which is very temperate) keeps the English order, at eleven o'clock, or soon after. In the afternoon commonly she visits, or is visited, by other ladies; but never goeth to sleep before she hath ended her office and ordinary devotions, which are many. You would say she were not only the great honour of her house but the glory of her country; and herein she shews herself to be truly the daughter of your noble grandmother, who shewed herself a lady of worthy example in all nobility and piety."

One more interview with the good duchess and we bring these introductory remarks to a conclusion.

In the year 1596, James the Sixth, king of Scotland, sent an embassy into Spain, under Robert, fourth lord Simpill, to congratulate king Philip the Third on his accession to the throne. The ambassador while at the Court became acquainted with the Duchess of Feria, whose letter to the king (dated at Madrid, 3rd June, 1600,) has been preserved in the Advocates Library at Edinburgh.[16] She reminds him of the dutiful affection which she bore to that blessed queen his mother, as also of the honour which she bears to his Majesty; in whom if she might also see her zeal in the Catholic religion, she professes she would be bounden to God for the hope she would receive by him for the repair of her wracks, both spiritual and temporal. She concludes with these words: "Wherefore I cease not to beseech daily the Almighty to illuminate your Majesty in that behalf, and to make you as great a saint on earth as was your blessed mother, to the advancement of His glory and good of our country."

Under the same date the duchess forwarded to King James certain "Reasons to intimate to the king's Majesty of Scotland whereby it may appear that his best way to obtain the crown of England is to become Catholic, and to give

[16] Numbered, MS. 33, 1, 10.

satisfaction thereof to the Catholics of England."

She premises that in England there are three sorts of men of different profession, namely, Catholics, Heretics and men of no religion, she continues her argument by remarking: that of these the "Catholics exceed in number either of the others; and of the three the zealous heretics are the most fervent; for the greatest part of all those that live in obedience to the Queen's laws are either dissembling Catholics or men of no religion, who would be as ready to follow a Catholic prince as an heretic, if occasion served."

So then, argued the duchess, if the King's Majesty of Scotland gained the Catholics, he consequently would gain the greatest part of those that are indifferent, or of no religion. For although some of them may be moved with particular affection to some pretender within the realm, yet the greater number of them will ever follow the strongest, which no doubt will be the king's Majesty of Scotland if the Catholics adhere to him; the other pretenders being divided amongst themselves.

The paper concludes with the following words of caution. "The Catholics, having noted His Majesty's education in heresy, his many actions conform to the same, the small satisfaction that he hath given to such as have sought his conversion, ascribe his moderate course used hitherto rather to policy than to any good inclination to the Catholic Faith. Therefore they cannot but think it dangerous to the Church of God and themselves to advance his title except they have assurance of his sincerity in religion; so that in the state that His Majesty now standeth, he cannot make any assured account to have any sufficient party in England."[17]

The text of the Life of the Duchess of Feria which forms the basis of the present volume was prepared for the press some years ago by the late Rev. E. E. Estcourt, Canon of St. Chad's Cathedral, Birmingham; who also at considerable expense collected a large amount of valuable material, illustrative of the incidents, persons and places which are mentioned in the narra-

---

[17] On Sempil's mission to Spain, see some additional details in Burton's History of Scotland, v. 286, ed. 1876.

tive.[18] The long illness and untimely death of the learned Canon prevented the appearance of his intended work in the form which had originally been announced. Now at length, after the delay of many years, the biographical narrative, as prepared by Canon Estcourt, is here issued by the present editor; but he has unwillingly been compelled to omit the many illustrative papers, pedigrees, drawings and other supplementary matter which had been brought together by the research and industry of the original Editor. The biography of the duchess as prepared by him for the press is here printed from his own transcript; and this little volume is now given to the public by the present Editor as a tribute to one whose loss he laments and whose memory he cherishes.

JOSEPH STEVENSON, S.J.

12th September, 1887.

[18] Here the present Editor cannot refrain from mentioning the existence at Grove Park of two admirable portraits of the Duchess of Feria. The first represents her as a young woman, in the pride of her beauty, and arrayed in all the splendour of the Court of Spain. In the second she appears in the plain and severe religious habit which she assumed on the death of her husband, and which she continued to wear during the remaining years of her widowhood.

AUTHOR'S PREFACE.

*TO THE RIGHT HONOURABLE HIS HONOURABLE
GOOD LORD, CHARLES DORMER, EARL OF
CARNARVON AND LORD BARON OF WING.*

*This treatise hath long lain by me, having dedicated
it to your honourable great-grandmother, my lady the
Lady Elisabeth Dormer, of happy memory. But
it having pleased Almighty God to take her to a
better world, where she enjoyeth the reward of her
virtuous life and her many good works, I did then
present it to your most noble and valiant father, who
in the penning of this Epistle died, to his eternal
honour and valour, in the service of his prince at
the battle of Newbury, this year 1643, professing his
happiness and content to die in the confession of the
Roman Catholic faith and performance to his duty
to his lawful king and sovereign. Your Lordship*

B

being kin of his house, and in confidence of his virtue and valour, I should have forgotten my duty, to have intituled it to any other, seeing the Lady Jane Dormer, Duchess of Feria, whose life and death it chiefly handleth, being so singular and renowned an honour to your noble family, and sister to my Lord Dormer your honourable great-grandfather.

In her Excellency your Lordship will behold a lively mirror of true Nobility, christian Piety, and illustrious Honour, an eternal worthy Pattern to your House and Posterity. In this treatise is also touched, as the course of the history occasioned, the the life of her virtuous Grandmother, the Lady Jane Dormer, and of her Saint-Brother, a Carthusian martyr, both of blessed memory; of the Lady Hungerford, Sister to my Lady Duchess; the life of the most excellent and pious Queen, Queen Mary, her Lady and Mistress; and the lives of both the Dukes, her husband and son. What is written here is out of approved histories, or from the relation of such persons against whose worth and credit no exceptions may morally be given; or from that which I myself have known, seen and heard. For my purpose and intention is to tell truth. To flatter, is either to gain, or to deceive; this is of vile and base negociants, the other of shifters and lewd companions, as Plutarch saith, the infamy of free men and custom of slaves. Extreme is the folly to use fiction where there is no necessity nor occasion; and to illustrate the honour and worth of so renowned and holy a personage with untruths, I hold it sacrilege; and to deprive her of right and due were apparent injury.

This history deserves a better and more learned pen; but I trust your Lordship will pardon defects, and accept in good part my good will in performing the duty, and obligation I owe to the happy memory of my most honourable good Lady and Mistress; and the serviceable respect and love I bear to your most noble House and Family, and in particular to your Lordship, whose life, health and happiness, may God Almighty bless with that prosperous increase of honours; as desireth your Lordship's most humble and affectionate servant,

H. CLIFFORD.

The Life of the Lady Jane Dormer, Duchess of Feria.

CHAPTER I.

THE DESCENT AND BIRTH OF THE LADY JANE DORMER.

THE Lady Jane Dormer was born of parents, whose progenitors have been of the most ancient nobility of England, and of worthy esteem, both in descent of blood, and effects of valour and virtue. The Cardinal Nicholas de Peleve, Archbishop of Rheims, and first Peer of France, well understood this, when, in the name of the Three Estates of that Kingdom, he answered the oration of the Duke of Feria, her son, who was Ambassador from Philip II. 2nd April, in the year 1593, to the League at Paris. " I cannot refrain," said the Archbishop " from mentioning your Mother,

who descended from the most illustrious Families
of England, daily bestows her bounty to relieve
and cherish the afflicted exiles for religion in
Spain, who are English, Irish, and Scots."

The family of Dormer, (as I have seen in an
old Pedigree, which is confirmed by tradition),
was anciently seated in Normandy, at the time
when King Edward the Confessor took refuge
there from the tyranny of Harold Harefoot, son
of King Canute, who had usurped the kingdom.
On being recalled from Normandy by Harold's
successor, Hardicanute, Prince Edward brought
in his retinue Thomas D'Ormer among other
Norman gentlemen, all of whom he advanced to
great places and dignities. The old tradition
saith, that in the wars which King Edward had
with the Danes and with Earl Godwin he was
much assisted with monies, which the said
Thomas D'Ormer lent him. And after a success-
ful end of these wars D'Ormer invited the King
to his house to dinner; which done, he brought
the tallies in a dish that were evidences of the
money which he had lent to the King, saying,
that for the hononr done his house, he had no
better dish to show his thankfulness withal, than
these wooden chips; and so he cast the tallies in-

to the fire. The King understood by the number
of the tallies the value of his debt, and the greatness of the gift, replied, with allusion to the
Etymology of his name, " Well mayst thou be
called D'Ormer, thou hast a sea of gold, doing
what thou hast done." In memory whereof it
is said, the Arms of Dormer were altered; for
whereas they formerly were a lion rampant, sable,
on a gold field, there was added, Azure, ten gold
Billets, and the lion placed in chief.[1]

Some may object, that neither the name of
Thomas Dormer, nor any such act of service is
found mentioned in any history; and that at that
time the usage had not begun of bearing arms to
distinguish families. But Stow in his English
Chronicle (p. 94.) recordeth, that King Edward
brought many out of Normandy, whom he promo-
ted to divers dignities, but nameth only two, who
were Churchmen. And of the many, why might
not Thomas Dormer be one? And in memory of
this service of Thomas Dormer to his King, some
succeeding Prince might grant his arms to be
honoured, as it is; divers Kings having done the

---

[1] Clifford here cites as his authority " P. Ribadeneyra in su
Epistola del libro de los Santos Estravagantes, dedicada a la
duquesa de Feria."

like to the posterity of them, who by their noble
exploits have well-merited of their country.

The son of this Thomas was William D'Ormer,
who joined with the Normans his countrymen,
when King William invaded England. His son
was likewise William, whose genealogy, in the
heir male hath continued in lawful succession
to this year 1616. The Lord Dormer that now
lives, being the only brother of the said Duchess
of Feria, among whose ancestors was Sir
William Dormer, who valiantly served King
Edward the Third in his wars against France
about the year 1350. Another, Geoffrey Dormer,
in King Henry the Sixth his days, had twenty-
six children, and most of them sons. But for the
particulars of progenitors, it is not my purpose
to rehearse, but only to discourse of such as
were concerned in the birth, education, and life
of the said Jane Dormer.

Robert Dormer, who was afterwards Sir
Robert, the grandfather of our Lady Duchess,
married Jane the daughter of John Nudigate of
Harefield in Middlesex, and Dame Amphyllis
Nevill of the house of Westmoreland. This Sir
Robert Dormer, a chief man of his country, a
great housekeeper, was beloved and honoured of

his neighbours. He was called by King Henry VIII. to be Treasurer of his army, wherewith the King went himself to Motterell in France. He was so beloved that the King, respecting his worth and valour, would have kept him at his court; but he returned into England voluntarily, retired to his house. Here he was contented to live among his neighbours, as his ancestors had done before him. For in those times good men of hospitality rather fled than followed high and ambitious titles. A further cause of his absence from the Court was first, the power and ambition of such as commanded, and afterwards, the King's disorder in questioning the lawful marriage with his good and virtuous wife Catharine. Proceeding to worse, came the grief that good Catholic men took for his departure from the obedience of God's Church, together with his violent persecution of such as constantly remained in the profession thereof; wherein this good knight shewed his zeal to God His truth. For when he saw the course and purpose of the King in his Parliament to carry all matters according to his passion, (which to crop or gainsay menaced utter ruin) he avoided by all

women, the wives of gentlemen of christian integrity, than of great ones, who were stained with the foul spots of such ungodly carriage. For to this end the Duke of Northumberland himself came once to his house of purpose to propound a match for one of his sons, and to make Sir Robert Dormer, (much beloved in his country,) a sure friend for his designs; but prevailed not.

This good knight, full of good works and zealous of God's honour, changed this mortal life for the immortal, in the year 1552; leaving the Lady Jane his widow, with whom he had lived forty years. It was she who was the bringer-up of her granddaughter, the Lady Jane; and was really more noble by her virtue and sanctity of life, than by birth, though descended of the Nevills of the royal house of Lancaster. She was grandchild to Sir John Nevill, her mother being his daughter and heir; and thus was descended of Thomas Nevill and Anne his wife, who was daughter to John Holland, Duke of Exeter, and Elisabeth his wife, the daughter of John of Gaunt.

The mother of Jane Dormer was the Lady Mary Sidney, eldest daughter of Sir William

Sidney, Governor and High Chamberlain of Prince Edward in the time of King Henry VIII. his Father; one of the heirs of Charles Brandon, Duke of Suffolk, being his cousin german.

Her brother was Sir Henry Sidney, who married Mary, daughter of the Duke of Northumberland, and was Lord Deputy of Ireland eight years. His daughter was the Countess of Pembroke, mother of Sir Philip Sidney.

Of Sir Henry's other sisters one married the father of the Lord Harrington; the third Sir William Fitzwilliams. The youngest, Frances, married the Earl of Sussex, Lord Chamberlain to Queen Elizabeth, and was the foundress of Sidney Sussex College in Cambridge. There were other two sisters, who died unmarried; both served the Lady Mary before she was Queen, and were much beloved by her for their rare virtue, and zeal in Catholic Religion.

Sir William Dormer by this his former wife had but these two daughters, Jane the subject of these memoirs, and Anne married to the Lord Hungerford. By his latter wife he had a son and three daughters, his son the now Lord Dormer, married Elisabeth, daughter of Antony, Viscount Montagu, and Magdalen his wife, daughter of the Lord Dacre of the North, through whom he allied his house with many noble families.

Sir William's eldest daughter by this wife was married to the son aud heir of the Viscount Montague, and is mother of Antony the now Viscount, a very Catholic and religious nobleman. His second daughter, Catharine, married the Lord St. John of Bletstoe; and his youngest daughter, Margaret, to Sir Henry Constable of the North, a very ancient and noble gentleman, whose son is the present Viscount of Dunbar, and married the sister of the Countess of Rutland.

CHAPTER II.

OF HER INFANCY AND EARLY YEARS. THE
HISTORY OF FATHER SEBASTIAN NEWDIGATE,
MARTYR.

JANE DORMER was born at Ethrop, not far from
Aylesbury in the County of Buckingham, in her
grandfather's house, on the 6th of January, the
year of our Lord 1538, being Sunday, and the
Feast of the Epiphany; therein presaging the
virtues of her after life by coming into the world,
when Christians were rejoicing in the birth of
our Lord.

In her baptism the name of Jane was given to
her after her grandmother; and this name signi-
fying grace, how well it did befit her will appear
in her life. When she began to speak and
discern, and learn her duty, her natural inclinations might easily be seen. She was apt, very
disciplinable, obedient, humble, awful, generous
in her condition; so that she seemed a child only
in years. She was much beloved by the servants

and gentlewomen, that were in her grandmother's house, (for there were many of noble descent, commended by their parents, to learn good education and virtue in that house), all presaging, that so sweet conditions, in so tender years and so graceful a countenance, gave hope to produce answerable effects.   So obedient a child was she to her parents and so subject to her tutress, as shewed plainly her good disposition and marvellous towardness. She was very forward to kneel upon her knees, to bless herself, to learn her prayers, to delight to go to the chapel, to have books and beads in her hands; and very prompt with contentment to all holy things. When she came to the age of four years, it pleased God to take her mother out of this world; that in her infancy the child might begin to taste the troubles and inconstancy of the world by so great a loss in a tender age. Her grandmother then took upon her the charge of bringing her up, and she was so rare and worthy a matron, there were few like her; of whose life and notable actions I shall record something.

The Lady Jane, daughter of John Nudigate, was married to Sir Robert Dormer in the year 1512. Of this marriage was born only one son,

Sir William. Before her marriage she was a mirror of recollection and devotion; as a wife, of modesty, prudence, and charity; as a widow, of patience, piety, and holy exercises. She was always a great friend of integrity; an enemy to vanity, very humble, severe to herself, fervent towards God, full of pity and compassion to the poor, and ever gracious and charitable to her neighbours and tenants. If any was sick, they were assured of her care and were cherished with good meats, and what else was necessary. Not only did she send daily to visit them, but she did not leave to see them herself, and succour their necessities; especially women in childbed. Even the poorest neighbour would she comfort with her presence, and with liberal hand she relieved them.

Such was the entire, chaste and true affection, wherewith she honoured and observed her husband, as she hath been known to affirm, that if he had died the very day of their marriage, she would never have married again. Such was her prudence, that he referred to her the government of his house and estate, which all his life she governed with great discretion and notable moderation. She brought up her son to fear God,

C

she so ordered her family, so took account of her
servants, and had care that all did their duty, as
it seemed that she had set before her eyes for her
guide and example the portraiture of "the valorous woman" painted by King Solomon. Always
she had a special eye to her maid-servants, that
they should keep home, be modest, shamefaced,
honest in behaviour. Her whole life praised her
memory. Herein were everywhere seen her
usual alms to the poor; her great charity to
priests, religious, and other distressed persons,
whom the impiety of the time persecuted; her
continual hospitality; her zealous counsels, and
Christian admonitions to her kin and friends
to persevere in the Catholic Faith; and her
care and diligence to remove from them all
hindrances, that might cool this perseverance.
Her women servants were relieved with honest
portions, some to marry, others to enter into
religion. Here too should be noted her accustomed bounty to the Church for the advancement
of God's service; her own labour and the labours
of her servants to work vestments, altar cloths,
and other ornaments for the same; her devotion
and fervour to the Catholic Religion in the time
of schism and apostacy by sustaining priests, not

only for her own house, but for the assistance and comfort of her neighbours; her hate of heresy; her hours spent in prayer and recollection; her works, her words;—all these things praise her and record her memory.

This Lady's brother, Sebastian Nudigate, was a gentleman of good parts, and of the Privy Chamber to King Henry the VIII., and not a little favoured by him. This king too much carried with his lustful appetites, began to be weary of his virtuous wife, and sensually to affect others. Hereupon this good Lady Dormer, fearing lest the bad example of so great a king should also corrupt her brother, invited him to her house, (which they make ordinarily a day's journey from London); discoursed with him of the alteration of the court; what was bruited in the country of the dissolute behaviour of the Courtiers; and the infamous example of the king, in rejecting so famous, noble and virtuous a Lady as the Queen was. She advised him to take heed of the deceits of the world, and the snares of the devil; to look to the duty of a Christian; and not to stain his soul and honour with so dangerous and pestilent contagions, as the bad example of so potent a master did lead him to. He replying, excused the king his master by saying that the report and her opinion of the king were worse than he demerited; but, if the king should prove so bad as the world suspecteth or speaks of him, Sebastian promised his sister to have in memory what she advised him. She answered, he should do well to remember it, and to perform it. "I shall," saith he. "I fear it," said she: At which word pausing a while, leaning his head upon his hand, he replied: "Sister, what will you say, if the next news you hear of me shall be that I am entered to be a monk in the Charter-house?" "A monk!" she saith. "I fear, rather, I shall see thee hanged. (Not many years after she saw both.) I pray God keep thee a good Christian; for such perfection is fit for men of other metal than loose Courtiers." So smiling her brother took his leave and returned to the Court.

The king went forward in his luxurious designs, advanced to dignities, and the greatest offices, corrupt and dissolute persons, such as flattered him in his unchaste and violent proceedings, abasing and displacing the worthy and virtuous. When Sebastian noted this with grief and trouble of mind, perceiving the horrible mists and tempests that these courses of the king did threaten

to the kingdom and reflecting upon the discourse
he had with his sister, he resolved to deliver himself from the snares of the Court, and the dangers of the world, and so as to betake himself in
time to a more secure harbour. Neither his
place in Court, nor the favour of the king, nor
his hopes of higher advancement did move him.
With a firm resolution he renounced all, and
entered Religion among the Carthusians in the
Charterhouse in London; a Religion, that in
England had especial veneration.

When his sister understood this she wondered
not a little that her brother should make so sudden a change, imagining it to be rather a delu-
sion, and temptation of the devil; first carrying
him to so high a pitch, and after to throw him
down. For this alteration on the sudden from
such delicateness, from such a place of ambition,
and liberty of conversation, to such austerity,
and despising of human glory, and recollection,
and strait silence, and perpetual clausure, bred
these fears in her mind. Albeit his inclination
was not of the worst, yet she held him no better
than others in the Court of honest name; never
dreaming of any such perfection, as that he
should enter an order so different from his bring-

ing up; for in his life, he could never digest fish, but if eaten, he would vomit it up again; and this order must never taste flesh.

Thus discussing with herself, she resolved to ride to London, to see him, and inform the Prior her opinion of it; so she took her journey, and came to the Charterhouse. She there desired to speak with the Father Prior, who coming to her, after due salutation, he heard her discourse of her brother. She advised the Prior to consider well the admittance of him into his order. For it seemed to her a thing unlikely, that one having to that time passed his life in wordly contentments, should on the sudden be fit for so strait and austere a religicn. The Prior answered, "Good Lady, thanks be to God, fit enough;" and that she should not trouble herself with this care. Her brother had passed his youthful years and was now a judicious man; he had well considered what he took in hand, and had already given sufficient proof, that the grace of God had moved and drawn him to this estate, and His Divine Providence had guided him to this order; and that from having been a remarkable courtier, he gave confidence to become a notable Carthusian. "If it be so," answered she, "blessed be

God, and blessed the day, in which he was born, that hath made so wise choice, so contrary to my opinion. I may then say, the happy lot is fallen upon him."

With that, the Prior commanded Brother Sebastian to be called ; who being come before his sister, tears gave her not leave to speak. It was not so much the alteration of his person and habit which did move her, as his gesture, his retired speech, his grave humility and modesty astonished her ; he so demeaning himself, as if he had been all his life in the monastery. With this she rested so content, as she could wish no more ; for this she reported herself. Growing more tender with this unexpected joy, she took her leave of the Father Prior, and the novice-monk, her brother, commending to Almighty God his perseverance in that happy estate, and herself, and hers to their good prayers. Worthy Sebastian went so forward, and profited in his religion and studies, as he took holy Orders, and was made Priest.

The king blinded with his sensual humour, made a quarrel against the Apostolic See, that would not give allowance to his divorce. He

attempted an utter breach, and disclaimed all
obedience, rending himself and the kingdom from
the unity of the Catholic Faith, and making it
high treason to acknowledge obedience to the
Apostolic See of Rome. Holiness of life now
began to be suspected as dangerous; religion
oppressed; good men evil entreated and afflicted;
and all things in a manner without term of reason
or justice in religious matters. When goodly
and virtuous men perceived and felt this, and
namely the Fathers of the Charterhouse; who
began to bewail the evils and miseries of the
times, (which never standing at a stay daily
spread further); they therefore did shortly expect
some sorrow to fall upon themselves in particular.
For, when the king had published that profane
and sacrilegious law,—commanding all to
acknowledge and to swear that he was the
Supreme Head of the Church within his Dom-
inions, (a law that was never heard of before in
any Christian Commonwealth) supposing, that
it would seem harsh to wise and intelligent men,
—he advised with his counsel; and resolved first
to draw to his will such as were of note, for
either their good life or learning. If these were

once gained, on whom the eyes of others were set, others might the more easily be brought and drawn to pretended submission.

Upon this device, having found by trial that fair promises and sweet persuasions prevailed nothing upon men constant in God's service, the king determined by violence and cruelty to force them to it. Whereupon, his wicked and sacrilegious ministers, set first upon the Fathers of the Charter House of London, in which monastery at that time were two other priors of the Carthusians, about business of the convents of their order; namely, Father Robert Lawrence, Prior of Beverly; and Father Augustine Webster, Prior of Hexham; with the Prior of the same house of London, Father John Haughton. All of these were very grave men, known to be men prudent, virtuous, and learned. With these three they first began by propounding to them the published edict of the King's Supremacy, to swear and subscribe to it. The venerable fathers answered: "This is a strange question to us, and unheard of before;" for that they had not read nor known the like example in the Church of God; which, in spiritual causes, is first to be heard, being the Spouse of our Lord Jesus Christ,

guided and directed by His Holy Spirit; to which
the laws of men ought to be subordinate. Sir
Thomas Cromwell (who was Vicar General for
the king in spiritual matters, and chief com-
missioner in this business) replied, reviling them
with very base and scurril terms, calling them
Knaves and Traitors in refusing it; and pressing
them to swear entirely and distinctly to all that
was demanded, whether the Law of God permitted it, or not permitted it.   The Fathers
excused it, saying : "that they were priests and
sons of the Catholic Church, whose doctrine
they must follow and obey Her precepts."   The
impious Vicar answered, "I have nought to do
with your Church; if you will not submit yourselves to the king's law, I will persecute you, and
your order, nor will I leave until I have destroyed
you all."   But these good Fathers, choosing
rather to displease the king than God, were with
two other priests, carried to prison; where after
much vile entreaty, and divers examinations,
they were brought after five days to the bar, and
condemned to death.   On the 4th of May in the
year 1535, they were in their religious habits
drawn to Tyburn, there hanged, cut down while
they lived, and quartered, and their quarters were

set upon the gates of the City, and those of the
Prior of London, upon the gates of his own
monastery.

Three weeks following, on the 25th of May,
when these cruel ministers of justice saw that
this savage handling of the foresaid fathers
availed nothing to quail or lessen the courage
and constancy of the rest, they took other three
prisoners of the house of London, Father Sebastian Nudigate, Father Humphery Middlemore,
Vicar of the convent, and Father William
Exmew, Procurator, both of them learned in the
Greek and Latin tongues, and greatly respected
in their order. Although they were not very
aged in years, yet they were ancient and reverent
in their deportment and of a gravity and holy
conversation. These three fathers they drew
out of the cloister with inhuman violence, led
them to the Marshalsea, where they kept them
fourteen days bound to pillars, standing upright,
with iron rings about their necks, hands, and
feet. This cruel usage was caused to force them
to yield to the king's pleasure, and to subdue
them, if possible, to subscribe to the law of his
supremacy. When the king understood their
constancy, supposing he had some interest in

Father Sebastian, he went disguised to the prison
to speak with him. He called for him, gave him
to understand the care he had of him, seeing he
came in person to visit him, and to advise him
not wilfully to destroy himself, knowing the
danger of the law, and what others of his profession had suffered for their contempt and
disobedience. He added the many graces and
favours he had done him; his ingratitude to be
of the number of those few, who, like traitors,
denied to conform themselves, as many others
both religious and all of the nobility had done;
which obstinacy could not be excused. He told
him that he was like to suffer greater torments
if he did continue in his folly and would not
apply himself to what he demanded, being bound
to obey his Lord and King, and do what he
commanded; "which, (saith the king) if thou
wilt do, thou shalt see that I have will to do thee
all favours, and power to accomplish them." A
mighty temptation and great encounter.

The good Father answered: "I must acknowledge this for a special and great honour,
yea far greater than my unworthiness can
deserve, that your Majesty hath vouchsafed, in
so undecent a lodging, to visit your poor servant,

and so poor a Religious. I confess I have
received many great favours of your Majesty.
God Almighty reward you, which I daily ask of
His Divine Màjesty; and I shall, while I live,
pray for your health and prosperity, and for the
happiness of your kingdom. I am a Religious
man, and therefore more obliged sincerely to
speak the truth. The desire to save my soul,
which our Lord Jesus Christ redeemed with so
great cost as the price of His Life, and the
shedding of His most precious Blood, insinuating
and dictating to my soul the hazards and dangers
of the world, to retire myself from them (otherwise my demerits might suddenly have overthrown
me) to this port of Religion, wherein I daily
commend, as all of our order do, the welfare
and life of your Majesty to Almighty God, to
multiply His graces towards you, and prosper
you with all desired felicity; taking the same
our Lord Jesus Christ for witness, that it is
neither contempt, nor obstinacy, nor discontent,
nor intent of gainsaying, nor counsel of any that
hath power to withdraw my submission to the
law, or to make me not to yield to the oath
propounded, but the doctrine of the Holy Church
and the Law of God, the offence whereof I may

not incur." The king would have no more; but went away in a great rage threatening and cursing.

After fourteen days that these good fathers had suffered this cruel torture, they were brought before certain Lords of the Privy Council, examined apart, and again demanded concerning this new Law of Supremacy, which, they said, had banished all foreign authority. Their answer was, "that the authority of the Church was not foreign in any Christian country; and that in no sort could they yield to any thing not agreeable to the Law of God, or contrary to the doctrine of our holy Mother the Church."

After divers examinations, promises and threats, finding them still constant, and that they could not be brought to any consent in this matter, they were sent as prisoners to the Tower of London, where they remained some eight days. The king being there, set again upon Father Sebastian, not with mild speeches as before, but with menaces and injurious words. Notwithstanding, this undaunted Confessor hears him with patience, and answereth: "When in Court I served your Majesty, I did it loyally and faithfully; and so continue still your humble

servant, although kept in this prison and bonds.
But in matters that belong to the Faith and
the glory of our Lord Jesus Christ, to the
doctrine of the Catholic Church and the salvation of my poor soul, your Majesty must be
pleased to excuse me." The King replies:
"Art thou wiser and holier than all the Eccle-
siastics and Seculars of my kingdom?" He
answered: "I may not judge of others; nor
do I esteem myself either wise or holy, being
far short in either; only this I assure myself
that the Faith and doctrine which I profess is
no new thing, nor now invented, but always
among the faithful, held for Christian and
Catholic. We must obey God rather than
man."

The king, having this resolute answer, would
not use further discourse, but called him traitor;
and, marvellously enraged, told him he should
suffer for such a one. No device or battery
could make any entrance into that valourous
breast armed with the Spirit of God, resting
immovable like a firm rock, remembering the
Divine counsel of the Psalmist: "Put not your
trust in princes nor in children of men, in whom
there is no salvation:" and like to that immortal

Macchabee who did not fear to say even to the face of King Antiochus: " We will not obey the king's precept, but the law of the Lord which is given unto us."

On the 18th of June, these three fathers were brought to Westminster to be tried before the Judges; where being indicted of high treason for refusing to subscribe and swear to the new-exacted oath of the King's Supremacy, they were again examined and demanded whether they would relent, and shew their obedience as other subjects did. They answered alike, that in that case, they neither could, nor would, nor ought to do it; citing and alleging divers authorities of the Divine Scripture, of the ancient Fathers, and of the Sacred Canons; proving and confirming that no temporal Prince can lawfully arrogate to himself the Church's government which the King of kings and Supreme Lord Christ Jesus gave and granted only to St. Peter and his Successors. They understanding and confessing this to be commanded by the Word of God, it were temerity and sin to go from this Faith, or to oppugn it. They were ready to have declared this with a grave and learned discourse if they had been permitted; still showing a firm resolution and valorous constancy in this doctrine. The Judges seeing no remedy, proceeded against them according to the form of their Laws, remitting them to a Jury of twelve men, by whom they were judged Guilty and convicted of high treason. But before the Judge would pronounce sentence of death, he used many reasons and persuasions now at last to yield and conform themselves; assuring them, upon submission, of the king's mercy, and withall wishing them to consider of the loss of so many good parts which might be serviceable to God and beneficial to their country. He spoke of the hastening of their end with an infamous death; the grief of their friends; the scandal of their kindred. In particular he addressed himself to Father Sebastian, repeating to him the nobility of his blood, the honourable allies he had in that kingdom, the duty he owed to his Majesty having been his servant; the many favours he had received from him; which if they would consider and be submissive, he did assure them there was place for mercy and pardon. But no persuasions could move minds so generous and so fixed in the love of God; who desired nothing more than to die for His cause, and to shed their blood for the

D

Catholic Faith. They made little reckoning of these vain and worldly considerations, and with great courage and constancy expected the sentence, which then was given in this manner: That they were found guilty of high treason, were to return to the place from whence they came and from thence to be drawn to the place of execution, where they were to be hanged; and then presently to cut the halter; their bowels to be pulled out; their bodies to be quartered and the quarters to be set up where the Justice should dispose them.

The Reverend good Fathers heard and received this cruel sentence, answering with alacrity of countenance " *Deo Gratias*," giving praise to our Saviour Jesus Christ for this gracious favour to make them worthy to suffer for His Faith and the defence of His Church. So they were returned to the prison: and the next day (the 19th of June) the sentence was executed. These blessed Fathers were then taken out of the prison, were laid stretched along bound upon hurdles and so drawn with horses through the streets of London to Tyburn, the place of execution. It was a lamentable spectacle to see innocent Religious men in their venerable habits, for profession of the ancient Catholic Faith to be thus handled by such as professed themselves Christians.

Being arrived at the place of execution, they praised Almighty God. They were patient to perform what the officers commanded; willingly and joyfully offering their bodies to that cruel and inhuman death for the honour of the Faith of Christ and the unity of His holy spouse the Church. No reason (for many were used and urged) availed to make any change in their minds or wills to obey the king's law. They untied Father Sebastian from the hurdle with the rope about his neck, put him in the cart; there he commended himself to the prayers of the good assistants; prayed for the king that God Almighty would give him long life and health, and His grace to have care of his salvation and of the good of his kingdom that had flourished so long in Christian Religion, and in the unity and obedience of Christ's Catholic Church. He intimated his own innocence both to the King and all the world, and that his death was only for the testimony and defence of the Catholic Faith, as their judges could do no less than testify. And so preparing himself to die said in Latin the

Psalm: " In Thee, O Lord, have I hoped, let me never be confounded," to the verse, "Into Thy Hands I commend my spirit: Thou hast redeemed me, O Lord, the God of truth." Then the cart being drawn away he remained hanging a very little or no space; for both he and the other two Fathers were cut down, being yet alive; presently bowelled; their bowels cast into the fire, their heads cut off, their bodies quartered and their quarters set up in the high ways and upon the gates of London. And in executing this barbarous cruelty upon such innocent persons, also was added this inhumanity, the second that was executed was made to stand to behold the death and the bloody slaughter of the first; and the third of them both, and this tyranny to see the bloody rending of their dear brethren.

This was the violent death but most happy end of Father Sebastian, an approved valorous gentleman, a perfect Religious, and a glorious Martyr of Christ Jesus. He was a singular honour of his house and an immortal renown of his family. For in nothing that doth illustrate the house of the Duchess (although descended from great Princes) is her blood more honoured than in this her kinsman and uncle, so illustrious

and famous a martyr, so worthy a Religious, and
so constant a servant of Christ Jesus; who in
the first risings and oppositions against the
Catholic Faith in our country so valiantly stood
for it, and for the defence thereof sealed it with
his blood and life.

This gentleman, as he has been described to
me, was somewhat tall of stature, his body well
proportioned and comely, his aspect lively and
settled. He had great courage; his behaviour
was pleasing, carrying it with a natural honesty
and remarkable modesty. But after that he
became a Religious, these parts of nature and
education were much magnified by those of grace
and piety, as hath been showed.

CHAPTER III.

OF THE GRANDMOTHER OF JANE DORMER. SHE
ENTERS INTO THE SERVICE OF THE PRINCESS
MARY.

THE elder sister of this glorious martyr was the
virtuous lady we now treat of, the grandmother
of the Duchess. Another sister was married to
Sir Leonard Chamberlain of Oxfordshire, mother
to the Lady Stonor, renowned for her zeal in
Catholic Religion, whom I saw, (being a boy), in
Oxford, convented there before the Judges for her
recusancy about the 23rd or 24th year of Queen
Elizabeth.[1] When she was reproved for her
constancy in the Catholic Religion, (which was
punishable by the laws of England,) she answered:
"I was born in such a time when Holy Mass
was in great reverence, and brought up in the
same Faith. In King Edward's time this
reverence was neglected and reproved by such as

---

[1] That is, about A.D. 1581 or 1582.

governed. In Queen Mary's, it was restored with much applause; and now in this time it pleaseth the state to question them, as now they do me, who continue in this Catholic profession. The state would have these several changes, which I have seen with mine eyes, good and laudable. Whether it can be so, I refer it to your Lordships' consideration. I hold me still to that wherein I was born and bred; and find nothing taught in it but great virtue and sanctity; and so by the grace of God I will live and die in it." This answer seemed to amaze the judges, spoken with great confidence; so they dismissed her upon ordinary sureties. This lady was generally noted for her rare devotion and marvellous abstinence, being widow even to her death.

Two other Sisters were Religious, one was Abbess of the Monastery of Sion by Brentford in Middlesex, who were of the holy order of St. Bridget, and yet continues entire in Lisbon and Portugal, brought out of England by the Lady Duchess when she came thence into Flanders; and there placed for some years until they removed to Spain. The other sister was of the order of St. Dominic. Both of them were exemplars for government and sanctimony of life. Two of their brothers were Knights of Rhodes, of the order and habit of St. John. In the year 1522 Rhodes was bravely besieged by Solyman, the great Turk, and valiantly defended by the Christian Knights of that Order, in which war both these brothers spent their lives.

The wisdom and virtue of Jane Dormer's grandmother were likewise well apparent in what she did, in marrying her son, Sir William. For when she saw the corruption of the state of this kingdom, and that those who by their authority and greatness should have been defenders of justice and religion, did seem to affect the contrary, her desire was to marry him with some virtuous gentlewoman answerable in quality. Sir Robert Dormer, her husband, liked it well, referring to her the charge of it, and wished her so to dispose it before the king should take notice of him, and hinder their intention by his command. For being their only child and heir to a great patrimony, many courtiers sought to him to marry their daughters with him, amongst whom Sir Francis Brien, a notorious favourite of the king; who much pretended to have him for husband to his niece, Jane Seymour. The power of this knight by his privacy with the king was great, whom to gainsay, there was more use of prudence than will, when he seriously treated the business of this marriage with Sir Robert Dormer, the father. In the interim that this treaty was entertained between them two, the mother, detesting the conditions of this knight, took her son and rode up to London to Sir William Sidney's house, having before made an overture to the Lady Sidney, who was well pleased. There the two ladies made up the match between the son of the one and the eldest daughter of the other. Which when Sir Francis Brien understood, seeing his pretence deluded was ill-pleased; but the lady took the business and blame upon herself, assuring him that she had treated the matter before with the Lady Sidney and could not go back. When he solicited the marriage for his niece, he sent them word that they should see his niece as well bestowed. For he, carrying her up to the Court, placed her with the Lady Anne Boleyn, the Queen, in whose service the king affected her, for which there was often much scratching and bye blows between the queen and her maid. In the end queen Anne Boleyn was imprisoned, condemned and beheaded for foul adultery. The next day after, the king married the Lady Jane Seymour, and had by her the king his son. The Lady Dormer in this prudent and valorous act shewing the singular affection that she had to piety and Christian Religion, and the respect she had to chaste and honest conditions, to have her son matched in a kindred of good fame, that neither the power of so great a favourite nor the gaining of so mighty a friend in Court, nor the present possession of a great dowry, nor the hopes of increase of honours, wealth and advancement by his means, nor the fear of inconveniences, that his displeasure might procure, could move this lady to marry her son with his niece who had made shipwreck of his Faith and honesty.

After King Henry died, when the child King Edward began to reign, the observance of Catholic piety was put to flight and abolished, as far as the public government could prevail, and heresy and schism brought in place. In order that it might take the deeper root, apostate priests and friars from foreign parts, with all their wives, were entertained in this kingdom, and sent to be public Preachers in the Universities, and to teach heresies. If any pious or learned Catholic gainsaid (as many did) the doctrine of these outlandish apostates, they were persecuted, put to silence, deprived of their livings, imprisoned, or banished. This good lady, grandmother to the Duchess of Feria, whose house was a refuge tb such persecuted men, gave them sustenance and security for their bodies; and received from them food and sustenance for the soul of herself, family, and neighbours. Notice hereof being taken by the Lady Mary, she did not a little favour her and hers, who, when she came to be Queen, this lady coming to her, she again remembered this hospitality, and very particularly thanked her for that charity, calling her the sustainer of the Catholic Faith. She, then commending to her Majesty divers of those good men, the Queen provided for all, entertaining some for her chaplains, and gave to others bishoprics, and other dignities. Such were the worthy persons to whom this good Lady gave hospitality.

If I should enter into particular discourse, what passed with this Lady in her charity and hospitality, it would contain many leaves of paper. For, wife and widow, being Lady of her

person and family, being renowned for her hospitality and christianity. They came not (as they said) to spoil or do any hurt, but to restore to the Commons that which was their own. Those great fellows, who without justice, and those rich ones, who without conscience, had appropriated to themselves what belonged to the people in common; these men were the marks they shot at; and they should suffer the penance of their cruelties and oppressions. And, as they promised, without doing any harm, more than going through her grounds and treading the grass, they marched forward, not doing nor offering the least occasion of wrong or offence to any person or goods belonging to her. Whereas in the parks and lands of the gentlemen round about her they made miserable spoil and committed many violences.

When it pleased God to take from this world Sir Robert Dormer, her husband, having been married about forty years, her son Sir William Dormer had been married to a second wife, after he had been widower nine years. He had by his first wife (as hath been said) only two daughters, and now had by this second a son, (who is now the Lord Dormer) who was of the age of five

months when his grandfather died.   This Lady
now a widow, being, disburdened of the obligations of a wife, did according to the counsel of
St. Paul, attend with more liberty to the service
of God.   In both estates she showed herself an
imitable pattern for noble women to follow and
a mirror to behold.   For, being married, she had
care, (as is shewed) to accomplish that which
appertained to the duty of a wife, by living
always in grateful love and due respect of her
husband; by governing her house in good order,
by directing her family with praiseable discretion,
by bringing up her son and grand-children (who
had lost their mother) in virtue; and in fine, she
behaved herself like a provident, wise and prudent lady and a careful good mother.   In her
widow's estate, she retired herself somewhat
more from the encumbring of worldly affairs,
retaining some care yet, as one well experienced,
of her son's estate.   She had her jointure and
living, severed from his, being sufficient and
answerable to the quality of the person, which
she well employed.   She spent much time in
prayer and devotion, and never failed, (having
health,) at divine service.   Her labours and

exercises were for the Church, and to do good to
such as were in necessity.

It was not long after the death of Sir Robert
Dormer, her husband, that King Edward died; to
whom succeeded the Catholic Princess, Queen
Mary, who obtained a renowned victory without
fighting or shedding much blood against the
Duke of Northumberland, who had set up his
daughter-in-law, the Lady Jane Grey.[2] In this
noise and tumult of war, to put down the right
Queen and maintain the usurper, Sir William
Dormer, this Lady's son, called friends and
gathered strength to assist Queen Mary. Upon
occasion, he went with them to Aylesbury, understanding that the Earl of Bedford would be there
with his adherents for the county of Buckingham
to proclaim the Lady Jane. Mr. Dormer encoun-
tering him there, told him plainly, " My Lord,
we cannot hear of any Queen but the Lady
Mary; and he that presumes publicly to name

[2] A proclamation of Jane Grey as Queen requiring the
persons therein addressed to proceed in her behalf to suppress
the advancement of Mary's supporters in Buckinghamshire,
may be seen in Hare. M.S. 416. fol. 30. It is dated at the Tower
of London, 18 July, in the first year of her reign. See the Chronicle of Queen Jane by J. G. Nichols, p. 109.

any other, shall do it to his cost." This so
affrighted the Earl that he durst not attempt
what was enjoined; and he retiring, Mr. Dormer
went with his friends and followers to attend
Queen Mary. This did he for his zeal to Right
and Justice, not respecting alliance or kindred,
for, his first wife, that was mother to the duchess,
was cousin german removed to the Lady Jane.
For this service and for the great charity of his
mother to Catholic learned men in King Edward's
days, (as hath been said) he was much favoured
by the Queen, who appointed him one of the six
Knights of the Bath in her coronation; she also
had his daughter the Duchess in her [service,
whom she much loved and esteemed, as hereafter
shall be more particularly declared.

In this Queen's reign, which was a few months
more than five years, this Lady remained with her
son, continuing her piety among her neighbours.
But when this virtuous and Catholic [Queen
died, there died with her the upholding of piety
and religion in England. For in the year 1558,
Queen Elizabeth succeeding, altered the government, entertained heresies; the defenders] of
them being her chief counsellors and commanders. This good Lady seeing this lament-

E

able alteration, although full of years, such was.
her zeal and love to the observance of true.
religion, as she left house, son, country, and
friends; choosing rather a banished life to serve
freely Almighty God than to remain in a kingdom
so perverted and corrupted. With this Christian
and zealous purpose in the year 1559, she passed
the seas`with her granddaughter, the Duchess
of Feria, into Flanders. And a little before the
Duchess parted from Mechlin for Spain, she went
to Louvain, there to keep a house and settle
herself; where resided many worthy and learned
English priests, exiled for not conforming themselves to the new and heretical injunctions of
England. There she lived the rest of her years
(which were about twelve) with so great fame of.
virtue, piety, charity, and other Christian works,
as not only that town and university but the
country about did much reverence and honour
her; and she is yet among the old people that
knew her, remembered with renowned com-
mendation. Yea, such were her works of
liberality and piety as the learned Doctor
Sanders in his book entitled "Visibilis monar-
chia Ecclesiæ,"[2] praiseth her as an eye-witness

[2] P. 708, ed. Lovan. 1571.

in these words: "The noble widow the Lady Jane Dormer, grandmother of the most illustrious Duchess of Feria, when she saw her country overrun by heresy, willingly exiling herself, hath so lived in Louvain for these twelve years as not only she hath kept herself from all schism, but also hath been a foot to the lame, an eye to the blind, a staff to the weak, a true mother of orphans, and a patroness of widows." Like another Dorcas she made many coats and garments for widows and poor people. When the Duke of Alva was general in those countries, his army was dispersed into divers towns, of whom there was a garrison of many soldiers in Louvain, who were pressed by necessity for want of clothes and meat. This good lady had provided in her house, a chamber which was fraught with cassocks, doublets, hose, stockings, hats and shirts, for poor soldiers, of whom, at a time, she had clothed forty soldiers and thirty soldiers.[8] Which, when the duke understood, he gratefully acknowledged the great obligations to her love and charity by giving her extraordinary privileges and exemptions for herself, house, and company. He esteemed her in that degree, that when the

[8] So the original

magistrates of Louvain pretended any suit from
the duke, they took this readiest means and help
by her assisting commendations, naming her
their patroness and protectress.

Always in the Holy Week on Maunday
Thursday, this lady called together twelve
widows, or rather poor women, washed their
feet herself, gave every one a new gown, a smock,
a little purse with money, and her dinner that
day, and on Easter day following. Her house
was a refuge and harbour for banished priests
and Catholic gentlemen of her country; many
poor students were daily relieved by her, as of
this day some living, in my hearing have given
grateful testimony.   People of all conditions
much respected her; the greatest of titles, lords
and ladies, often visited her, and had her in
especial regard. The university and town of
Louvain honoured her exceedingly, as the many
courtesies she received from them in life, and the
honour they did her after her death do well
testify.

In the year 1571, the 7th of July, this lady
(being about eighty years of age), left this natural
life to live for ever with God Almighty. After
having received with great devotion the holy

Sacraments of the Church, she remained to the
last hour in good sense, and judgment, with great
quietness and security of conscience. She had
ordained her testament; bequeathed large alms
to the poor, to colleges, to Religious, both men
and women, of sundry monasteries; had left her
lands and rents to her son as heir of them, and
the goods that remained, absolutely to the disposing of the duchess, her grand-daughter, to
whom her affection was ever most particular;
for naming her or writing to her, still used this
term: "My most dear and beloved daughter;"
as appears in her will, the copy whereof I have.
Her soul she commended to Him Who created
and redeemed it; which, so full of good works no
doubt and abounding with so many pious and
Christian deeds of exemplar charity, ascended to
Him without stay, as may morally be believed.

Her body when it was buried, was done with
the solemnity fitting her quality. Many orphans,
widows, and poor people according to her testament, were clothed, who attended the funeral.
The prelates, doctors, regents, and chief of the
university, the religious of all Orders, did go in
their places. The gentlemen and magistrates of
the town, accompanied likewise in their rank,

with the rest of the mourners to the church of the Charter-house, where she was buried. And the next day following, a great number of the poor of the town (an example seldom seen, and worthy the consideration) assembled together at this lady's house; and every one, a candle lighted in their hands, went in orderly procession, the way that her body was carried the day before, to the Charter-house, bewailing their loss, and praying for her soul. Which action of their memorable love came from their own motive and gratitude.

She was buried, as I say, in the church of the Charter-house (where she could not be admitted in life by reason of her sex) in the middle of the choir, just before the High Altar; where also lieth buried with her, the body of the Lady Anne Hungerford, her grand-daughter, only sister by father and mother to the duchess, who thirty-two years after died in the same town of Louvain, and there both lie reconded under a fair marble tomb, underset with marble pillars; their portraitures cut very lively in alabaster at length lying upon the top. Epitaphs and escutcheons of their descent and matches were erected at the cost of the duchess, with an annual rent for ever of a hundred florins given by her to the same Charter-house paid out of the Town house of Antwerp.

This Lady Hungerford, the year that her grandmother died, came out of England, being over the seas, before she understood of her death, whose Catholic piety and noble desires could not content her husband, Sir Walter Hungerford ; who albeit nobly descended, yet by base covetousness and disordered sensual living much blemished his person and worth. He did not entreat his lady as was due to his wife and a gentlewoman of her rank, whereupon she pretended his leave to go beyond seas to her grandmother, where she might have liberty of conscience and serve God freely. In this he, to have more liberty for his sensual appetites, and to avoid the troubles for her conscience, not unwillingly consented; and so, as I say, she passed to the Low Countries where she lived thirty-two years, with great example of true nobility and Christianity, much honoured for her rare parts of valour, and discretion, the memory whereof remains in Namur and Louvain, in which places she for the most part lived. Madam Margaret of Austria, Duchess of Parma,

sister to King Philip II. of Spain, then Governess
of these provinces for her brother, took much
contentment in her conversation, knowing her to
be the duchess' sister, honoured her with very
special affection, invited her often, commending
to divers her noble behaviour and the worth of her
parts such as she knew in very few women; as
the party who heard her highness speak it, told
me. The governors and magistrates of the
towns where she lived in all imminent dangers
(for then the war in those parts was hot) took
particular regard to her, came to her house, presented all the security they could for her person,
goods, and family; thereby assuring the great
care they had of her safety. Such was the merit
of her carriage. And when fears or dangers
occurred, her courage and magnanimity were
rare and generous. To gentlemen distressed and
poor students, her liberality was marvellous,
always compassionate, a great alms-giver. In
this her exile she had the grief to lose her only
son in the flower of his youth, in the state to
marry, a gentleman of great hopes, very noble in
condition, discreet and virtuous. A chastisement
which Almighty God lays upon adulterers, from
which crime, I wish his father had been innocent:

so his house might have continued in his blood, which now is dispersed.

This Lady Hungerford passed out of this world on the 19th of December, 1603, full of good works, imitating the steps of her worthy grandmother.[4]

In testimony of the worth and great merits these two ladies, not only the ordinary but the public voices of the country proclaim it, and such as served them many years; but the writings and assertions of the principal and most learned of our nation, then beyond the seas, do avouch the same; as for example that grave and learned Prelate, Dr. William Allen, afterwards Cardinal, Dr. Owen Lewis, Bishop of Cassano, Dr. Nicholas Sanders, Dr. Thomas Stapleton, both great writers and public readers of Divinity and others, to the number of fifty, who were petitioners to Pope Gregory the XIII., to procure the duchess to be sent to the Low Countries. They, when treating the business with Cardinal Morono, their patron in the Court of Rome, and Protector of the English nation,

---

[4] The MS. here gives ten lines of Latin poetry, being a copy of the verses engraven "at the fore-end of her tomb."

among other reasons that they allege in a common letter, dated 28th December 1572, mention divers [5] favours, received from the duchess.

CHAPTER IV.

OF THE YOUTH AND EDUCATION OF JANE DORMER.

JANE DORMER, brought up under so worthy a matron, in her infancy, beginning to be of understanding, the first thing she learned was her duty to serve God, and her obedience to her father, grandfather, and grandmother, by conforming herself with affectionate humility to their commands. This virtue she so embraced, as with rare respect it continued with her, even to the death of her grandmother, although exalted to a higher rank. And when she served Queen Mary, being of her bedchamber, she never neglected her duty and obedience to her grandmother, never would do any matter of moment, without making her acquainted, and asking her

[5] " Dr. Sanders was the bearer of this letter." MS.

leave; and what she was commanded or advised by her, that did she carefully obey.

Before seven years she began to read the Primer, or as we call it, the Office of our Blessed Lady, in Latin; and from that time, daily continued it, having any possibility of health to the end of her life, which was sixty-seven years. In such curious works of the needle as gentlewomen learn, she attained a marvellous skill and perfection. For I have seen samplers, and divers of her works, wrought with her own hands, very curious, rare, and excellent, so adjudged by such as were held great mistresses in such works. Also divers dressings for the altar, and ornaments for the priests and such as serve at the altar, very rich and sumptuous, of notable invention and variety, all wrought by herself. Together with these abilities, she always retained a commendable modesty in all she did or spake.

Her grandfather Sir William Sidney, whom the king, though still carried away by his own exorbitant passions, did choose to be tutor and governor of his son Prince Edward, when remaining for a time at Ashridge, (which was not far from her grandfather Dormer's) sent for her to entertain some time with the prince. They were both near of one age, about six or seven years, the prince being only elder by three months; he desired her company, taking particular pleasure in her conversation. Thither she was sent with her governess, passing her time with the prince, either in reading, playing, or dancing, and such like pastimes, answerable to their spirits and innocency of years, and in playing at cards, would use this speech, as it fell out: "Now Jane, your king is gone, I shall be good enough for you."

I have heard them that were about the prince avouch it, that his inclination and natural disposition was of great towardness to all virtuous parts and princely qualities; a marvellous sweet child, of very mild and generous condition. Afterwards, when his father died, (he being but nine years of age), mischievous and heretical governors, contrary to his father's will, abused his tender age; who ruling to effect their own ends notoriously injured the natural good inclination of this gentle and noble prince. For, when he was king, in passing by the ruins of goodly monasteries, he demanded what buildings were those? It was answered: That they were religious houses, dissolved and demolished by order of the king his father, for abuses. He replied: "Could not my father punish the offenders, and suffer so goodly buildings to stand, being so great an ornament to this kingdom; and put in better men, that might have governed and inhabited them?" seeming to lament that lamentable course. And when the Lady Mary, his sister, (who ever kept her house in very Catholic manner, and order) came to visit him, he took special content in her company (I have heard it from an eye-witness) he would ask her many questions, promise her secrecy, carrying her that respect and reverence, as if she had been his mother. And she again in her discretion, advised him in some things that concerned himself, and in other things that touched herself; in all shewing great affection and sisterly care of him. The young king would burst forth in tears, grieving matters could not be according to her will and desire. And when the duke his uncle did use her with straightness and want of liberty; he besought her to have patience until he had more years, and then he would remedy all. When she was to take leave, he seemed to part from her with sorrow; he kissed her, he called for some jewel to present her, he complained that they gave him no better to give her. Which noted by his tutors, order was taken, that these visits should be very rare, alleging that they made the king sad and melancholy; and consulted to have afflicted her officers and servants; for that contrary to the then made law, she had public Mass in her chapel, if they could draw any assent from the king. But he, upon no reasons, would ever give way to it, and commanded strictly that she might have full liberty of what she would. He sent to her, inquiring if they gave her any trouble or molestation, for if they did, it was against his will, and he would see her contented. But it was not safe, nor did it stand with prudence, as the times went, for the Lady Mary to complain.

When Jane Dormer grew older, she was commended by her grandmother to the most noble and Catholic princess the Lady Mary, so persuaded by her grandfather Sidney, whom two of his daughters had served before and died in her service, much favoured by her Highness for their virtue. When the queens (the wives of King Henry) had sought with much importunity to have them in their service they would by no means leave the Lady Mary although the king

himself requested it.[1] In those days the house
of this princess was the only harbour for honour-,
able young gentlewomen, given any way to piety
and devotion. It was the true school of virtuous
demeanour, befitting the education that ought to
be in noble damsels. And the greatest lords in
the kingdom were suitors to her to receive their
daughters in her service.

With the Lady Mary, Jane remained after the
time, when by the death of King Edward the
kingdom fell to her, and even till her decease out
of this world. And being in her service was
particularly favoured by her and affected; with
which she corresponded with all dutiful respect,
so as seldom or never would the queen permit
her absence. She slept in her bedchamber, many
times with her; she read together with her our
Lady's Office; she committed to her charge and
trust her usual wearing jewels and what else was
of esteem to be commended to one of her bed-
chamber. At table, she eat the meat that the
hand of Jane Dormer carved for her, which is an
evident argument and proof of her virtues when

[1] Ladies of the name of Mabel and Elisabeth Sydney are
mentioned in Queen Mary's Household Book, pp. 119, 126, 184.

so virtuous a princess, and of so admirable parts did so much favour and esteem her.

This queen seldom went in progress except it were to the Cardinal's house at Croydon (for Cardinal Pole her kinsman was Archbishop of Canterbury) avoiding by all means to trouble and grieve her subjects in time of hay and corn harvest, when they had use of their horses and carts. And being at Croydon, for her recreation, with two or three of her ladies, she would visit the poor neighbours, they all seeming to be the maids of the Court; for then she would have no difference, and ever one of these was Jane. She would sit down very familiarly in their poor houses, talk with the man and the wife, ask them of their manner of living, how they passed, if the officers of the Court did deal with them, as such whose carts and labours were pressed for the queen's carriages and provisions.[2] And among others, being once in a collier's house, the queen sitting by while he did eat his supper, on her demanding the like of him, he answered, that they had pressed his cart from London, and had

[2] Various illustrations of Queen Mary's kindness and liberality towards the poor may be seen in her Privy Purse Expenses printed by Sir F. Madden. See p. 258.

not paid him. The queen asked if he had called
for his money. He said, yea, to them that set
him awork, but they gave him neither his money
nor good answer. She demanded; "Friend," is
this true, that you tell me?" He said, "Yea,"
and prayed her to be a mean to the comptroller,
that he and other poor men might be paid. The
queen told him she would, and willed that the
next morning about nine or ten o'clock, he should
come for his money. She came no sooner to the
Court, but she called the comptroller,[8] and gave
him such a reproof for not satisfying poor men,
as the ladies who were with her, when they heard
it, much grieved. The queen said that he had
ill officers who gave neither money nor good
words to poor men, and that hereafter he should
see it amended, for if she understood it again,
he should hear it to his displeasure; and that
the next morning the poor men would come for
their money, and that they should be paid every
penny. Mr. Comptroller wondered how this
came to the queen, and the ladies told him what
had passed that evening.

[8] Probably Sir Robert Rochester, who was appointed by the
Queen at her accession and continued in office till his death in
December, 1557, or Sir William Kingston, who died in 1541.

F

In the visiting of these poor neighbours, if she found them charged with children, she gave them good alms, comforted them, advising them to live thriftily and in the fear of God, and with that care to bring up their children; and if there were many children she took order they should be provided for, placing both boys and girls to be apprentices in London, where they might learn some honest trade, and be able to get their living. This did she in a poor carpenter's house, and the house of the widow of a husbandman. And in this sort did she pass some hours with the poor neighbours, with much plainness and affability; they supposing them all to be the queen's maids, for there seemed no differnce. And if any complaints were made she commended the remembrance very particularly to Jane Dormer.

CHAPTER V.

THE MARRIAGE OF JANE DORMER WITH THE DUKE
OF FERIA. SKETCH OF THE LIFE AND
CHARACTER OF QUEEN MARY.

THESE special favours that the queen shewed to
Jane Dormer, together with the rare parts of her
mind and person, were occasion that divers of
the greatest worth and nobility did seek her for
marriage; as Edward Courtenay, Earl of Devonshire, son of the Marques of Exeter, and cousin-
german removed of the queen, whom the queen
delivered from the Tower at her entrance there,
at the same time with the other prisoners, the
Duke of Norfolk, and the Bishops Bonner,
Tunstall, and Gardner. This last bishop would
have made the match, finding the Earl to have
an affection to her; and some were of opinion he
did it to prevent his marriage with the Lady
Elizabeth, whereof afterwards grew the greatest
part of her troubles in Queen Mary's time. He

did solicit the queen about the match, and dealt with the young lady, to have it effected. Also the Duke of Norfolk was a suitor to her, being at that time the only duke in England, and some others of great quality, which the Duke of Feria afterwards confesseth in his last will, making a petition for her to the king, tells him that she had refused greater matches than himself in her own country. The Earl of Nottingham that now is Lord Admiral, being of her years, and in that time calling her mistress, told me, when he was ambassador in Spain, in 1605, that she was the fairest and the sweetest woman of the world; and that the whole Court did admire her, and bear her a reverent respect, as well for her own worth, as for the esteem the queen did bear her. But Jane in these pretences would do nothing, without the consent of her Majesty, who had no great will to leave her, and would say in the treating of these matters, that Jane Dormer deserved a very good husband; and would add further, that she knew not the man that was worthy of her. When it chanced that Jane was not well, as that she could not well attend upon the queen, it is strange the care and regard her Majesty had of her, more like a mother or sister

than her queen and mistress. As in the last
days of this blessed queen, she being at Hampton
Court, and to remove to London, Jane having
some indisposition, her Majesty would not suffer
her to go in the barge by water, but sent her by
land in her own litter, and her Physician to
attend her. And being come to London, the
first that she asked for was Jane Dormer, who
met her at the stairfoot, told her that she was
reasonably well. The queen answered " So am
not I," being about the end of August, 1558. So
took her chamber, and never came abroad again.

At that time the king was in Flanders about
his wars, made upon the frontiers of France, who
understanding the Queen's sickness, being then
with his army before Dourlens,[1] sent away the
Duke of Feria, to serve and assist her in all that
should be requisite. It pleased Almighty God,
that this sickness was her last, increasing daily,
until it brought her to a better life. Jane was
continually about the Queen, not yet married, for
the Queen would not have her marry, until the
king was returned from Flanders ; which occasioned the want of great gifts and rich endow-
ments wherewith the Queen had determined and

[1] A fortified town, about eighteen miles north of Amiens.

promised to honour the marriage, whereof did her Majesty complain. She finding herself languishing to death, told Jane, she would have been glad to have seen her marriage had been effected in her days; but God Almighty would otherwise dispose, and being sick and the king absent, she was not in case to do what she would. Her sickness was such as made the whole realm to mourn, yet passed by her with most Christian patience. She comforted those of them that grieved about her; she told them what good dreams she had, seeing many little children like Angels play before her, singing pleasing notes, giving her more than earthly comfort; and thus persuaded all, ever to have the holy fear of God before their eyes, which would free them from all evil, and be a curb to all temptations. She asked them to think that whatsoever came to them was by God's permission; and ever to have confidence that He would in mercy turn all to the best.

From the time of her Mother's troubles, this queen had daily use of patience and few days of content, but only those that she established and restored the Catholic Religion to her kingdoms. While she was queen, in those few years, she suffered many conspiracies, and all out of mali-

cious humours to God's truth. She gave commandment to all, both of her Council, and servants, to stand fast in the Catholic religion ; and
with those virtuous and Christian advices, still in
prayer and hearing good lessons, receiving the
holy Sacraments of the Church, left this world,
which was the 17th day of November, 1558. That
morning hearing Mass, which was celebrated in
her chamber, she being at the last point (for no
day passed in her life that she heard not Mass)
and although sick to death, she heard it with so
good attention, zeal, and devotion, as she answered in every part with him that served the
Priest ; such yet was the quickness of her senses
and memory. And when the Priest came to that
part to say, *Agnus Dei, qui tollis peccata mundi*, she
answered plainly and distinctly to every one,
Miserere nobis, Miserere nobis, Dona nobis pacem.
Afterwards seeming to meditate something with
herself, when the Priest took the Sacred Host to
consume it, she adored it with her voice and
countenance, presently closed her eyes and rendered her blessed soul to God. This the duchess
hath related to me, the tears pouring from her
eyes, that the last thing which the queen saw in
this world was her Saviour and Redeemer in the

sacramental species; no doubt to behold Him
presently after in His glorious Body in heaven.
A blessed and glorious passage. *Anima mea cum
anima ejus.*

This good queen had commended in private
divers things to Jane Dormer to give to the Lady
Elizabeth her sister, and to tell her who was to
succeed her in the kingdom; which she performed
with dutiful fidelity, giving her the rich and precious jewels, that were in her custody,[2] which
Queen Elizabeth willingly received, and sent her
messages. These were to uphold and continue
Catholic Religion, to be good to her servants,
and to pay what might justly be required. But
this of religion, I know not what reasons of base
moment, or other circumstances of devilish
policy had diverted her herein; notwithstanding
before in the queen's sickness, she had faithfully
promised the continuance; and all the reign of
Queen Mary, the Lady Elizabeth did hear daily
two masses, one for the living, another for the
dead, seeming extraordinary devout to our Blessed
Lady; and in her troubles being examined about
religion, she prayed God, that the earth might

[2] The delivery of the jewels is the subject of two memoranda
in the Record Office, Domest. Eliz. VIII. 24.

open and swallow her up alive, if she were not a
Roman Catholic. And this is likewise confirmed
by the duke of Feria his letter to the king, who
in this sickness of the queen visited the Lady
Elizabeth, certifying him, that she did profess
Catholic Religion, and believed the Real Presence, and was not like to make any alteration
for the principal points of religion.

I will now speak somewhat of these two
queens' births. And then of other passages of
their lives, whereof only the truth shall be
written, and most out of the testimonies of
protestant writers.

Queen Catharine was some five years older
than the king, and very different in manners.
She rose at mid-night to be present at the matins
of the Religious. At five o'clock she made herself ready with what haste she might, saying
that the time was lost which was spent in ap-
parelling herself. Under her royal attire she did
wear the habit of St. Francis, having taken the
profession of his Third Order. She fasted all
Fridays and Saturdays and all the Eves of our
Blessed Lady with bread and water. On Sundays she received the Blessed Sacrament, read
daily the Office of the Blessed Virgin, she was

the most part of the morning in the Church at
holy service and after dinner read the life of that
day's Saint to her maids standing by.   Then she
returned to the Church.   She was sparing in her
supper.   She prayed kneeling on her knees without cushions.   She was affable in conversation,
courteous to all, and of an excellent and pious
disposition.   This lady, a mirror of goodness,
was afterwards brought into infinite troubles, so
to be tried as that the sweet savour of her virtues
might be diffused over the whole christian world.

Henry the Eighth, weary (as it seems) of this
good queen Catharine, after fifteen years' co-habi-
tation, by the suggestion of Cardinal Wolsey begins
to make scruple whether this marriage with the
Lady Catharine was lawful, for that she had been
before his brother's wife.   Pope Julian the second
gave lawful dispensation to make good the
marriage.   That learned and glorious martyr
doctor John Fisher, the light not only of the
kingdom of England but of the whole Christian
world, when this divorce was in pleading, delivered to the legates a paper most learnedly written
in defence of the marriage, advising them not to
seek a knot in a rush nor to suffer the manifest
truth of Holy Scripture and Ecclesiastical laws,

sufficiently seen and examined in this cause, to be perverted; but rather to consider again and again how great mischiefs would follow by this divorce, to wit, hatred between King Henry and Charles the Emperor, and the factions of the princes who would join them. And the most grievous of all,—dissensions in matters of faith, schisms, heretics and infinite sects. " I (said he) have in this matter laboured much and employed my utmost industry; and I dare affirm what I have not only proved in this writing, and clearly taught by the testimony of the Sacred Scriptures and of Holy Fathers, but also am ready to testify it with the shedding of my blood, that there is no power on earth that can dissolve or disjoin this marriage, which has been joined by God Himself."

This with other learned and pious writings that the other advocates did present to the legates, although Cardinal Wolsey was one, did move them not to give sentence as the king desired and required; nor would Clement VII., then Pope, give way to it, who then being at war with the emperor was offered by King Henry to maintain four thousand [men] in his wars against Cesar. So much did he desire this divorce to marry the Lady Anne Bullen. He sought all means by gifts and corruptions to most Universities to have their favourable opinions for this his desire. Cardinal Wolsey had it intimated, in regard to his note to the emperor, that the king might marry with the Lady Margaret, a very fair woman, the widow of the Duke of Alençon and sister to Francis, the French king.

Thomas Cranmer, chaplain to Sir Thomas Bullen, the supposed father of the Lady Anne, was a man to the king's own heart. He turned as the king pleased, flattered and followed him in all his demands. He pronounced the sentence of divorce by which Queen Catharine was to be called the princess dowager of Prince Arthur and Anne was to be held lawful queen.

Mr. Camden conceals the time of the marriage of Anne Bullen, for that the Lady Elizabeth's birth was in four months after. I marvel that he tells not the time of the king's espousals with her, nor of her marriage and her coronation, she being the mother of her whose life and reign he published. He says only that she was born 7th September, 1533, at Greenwich. Queen Catharine was banished from the Court to Kimbolton, where living retired with her maids until 6th January, 1536, she left this mortal life. It is said that her days were shortened by the intemperature of the unwholesome air, but chiefly by the continual increase of griefs and calamities; and some were of opinion, not without suspicion of poison, for the Lady Anne hated her extremely. When the king understood her death he shed tears and commanded all his household to wear mourning; but his new wife did clothe herself in yellow, glad of her death that she died so quietly. Her body was buried at Peterborough. She never could be persuaded after her banishment from the Court to enter into a monastery, although most desirous of that life, nor to do anything that might be in prejudice of her marriage, although exposed to many injuries and manifest dangers. Nor could she be drawn to go into Spain, or into Flanders, whither she was invited by the emperor, her nephew, where she might have had most honourable entertainment. She applied these miseries and disasters to have specially happened for the death of Prince Edward Plantagenet, son of the Duke of Clarence, brother to King Edward the Fourth; whom (most innocent) Henry VII. put to death to make the kingdom more secure to his pos-

terity, and to induce King Ferdinand to give his
daughter, this Catharine, in marriage to Prince
Arthur. Before her death she wrote two pious
letters, one to the king, the other to Friar Foster,
her ghostly father, then in prison, after with
cruel tortures a glorious martyr. Thus ended
this great queen and holy princess, renowned in
all nations and magnified by most writers of
those times.

Within five months after, Queen Anne was
brought to her reckoning for another world, but
after a different life to her predecessor. It was
passed most in masks, dancing, plays and such
corporal delights, in which she had a special
grace,—temptations to carnal pleasures and inventions to disgrace such and ruin them who
were renowned for virtue. From the time that
Queen Catharine was defended so stoutly and
learnedly by the Bishop of Rochester she did
seek by all means his destruction. One Richard
Rice, a cook, was suborned to poison him, and he
knew no other way to do it than to poison the
common pot, which was for the whole household
of the bishop. It chanced that that day according to his custom the bishop came not to dine in
the parlour, but most of his family that dined

there were poisoned and died thereof. Rice the cook being discovered did confess it and was publicly put to death for it. And when a gentleman brought word to the king that Sir Thomas More was then beheaded, the king being at table, and the Lady Anne standing by, the king throwing away the dice showed anger and sorrow that he was troubled and said to her, " This is long of you; the honestest man of my kingdom is dead," and suddenly retired chafing.

But to come to her death. The king seeming to affect Jane Seymour, and having her on his knee, as Queen Anne espied, who then was thought to be with child, she for anger and disdain miscarried, as she said, betwitting the king with it, who willed her to pardon him, and he would not displease her in that kind thereafter. But the queen, much wanting to have a manchild to succeed, and finding the king not to content her, to have her purpose did accompany with her own brother, Lord George Bullen, Viscount Rochfort, Francis Weston, Henry Norris, William Brereton and Mark Sweton, a musician, all of the Privy Chamber, for which they all suffered death. Three days after that Anne Bullen herself was beheaded on 14th May,

1536, the Duke of Norfolk sitting High Steward.
She was convicted and condemned by twenty-six
peers, whereof her father was one, who shortly
after died of grief. She was not twenty-nine
years of age. We see how different were the
mothers of these two queens, and of the latter
the father might be doubted, for Queen Mary
would never call her sister, nor be persuaded she
was her father's daughter. She would say she
had the face and countenance of Mark Sweton,
who was a very handsome man. But we will
pass to their education.

To speak briefly of the education and some
passages of the life of Queen Mary, I should
relate that she was bred under her virtuous
mother, as well in princely splendour, as in true
piety, to know and serve Almighty God and to
have His holy fear before her eyes; and afterwards
was commended for her further education to the
Countess of Salisbury, the mother of Cardinal
Pole, and cousin german to the queen her grandmother, a most pious and saint-like woman.
She was declared Princess of Wales and heir
of the kingdom ; so bred as she hated evil ; knew
no foul or unclean speeches, which when her lord
father understood, he would not believe it but

would try it once by Sir Francis Brian, being at a mask in the court; and finding it to be true, notwithstanding, perceiving her to be prudent and of a princely spirit, did ever after more honour her. It chanced once that she and the Lady Anne Boleyn at Eltham, heard Mass together in one room. At the end of Mass, the Lady Mary made a low courtesy and went to her lodging; so did the Lady Anne, then called queen. When she came to her quarter, one of her maids told her that the Lady Mary at parting made reverence to her, she answered that she did not observe it; and said, "If we had seen it, we would have done as much to her;" and presently sent a lady of honour to her, to excuse it; adding, that the love of none should be dearer nor more respected than hers, and she would embrace it with the kindness of a true friend. The lady that carried the message came when the Lady Mary was sat down at dinner. When admitted, she said; "The queen salutes your grace with much affection and craves pardon, understanding that at your parting from the oratory, you made a courtesy to her, which if she had seen, she would have answered you with the like; and she desires that this may be an entrance of friendly corres-

G

pondence, which your grace shall find completely to be embraced on her part." "It is not possible," answered the Lady Mary, "that the queen can send me such a message; nor is it fit she should, nor can it be so sudden, her majesty being so far from this place. You would have said, the Lady Anne Boleyn, for I can acknowledge no other queen but my mother, nor esteem them my friends who are not hers. And for the reverence that I made, it was to the altar, to her Maker and mine; and so they are deceived, and deceive her who tell her otherwise." The Lady Anne was maddened with this answer, replying, that one day, she would pull down this high spirit.

Ludovicus Vives[1] dedicated to her in the year 1524, two hundred and thirteen *Symbola,* or short and intricate sentences, in few words, which we call commonly Mottoes, with paraphrasing upon every one of them. The first was, *Scopus vitæ Christus;* the last was, *Mente Deo defixus.* These she seemed to have in perpetual memory, by the practice of her whole life; for she made Christ the beginning and end of all her actions, from Whose goodness all things do proceed, and to

In his Epistle to the Lady Mary, from Eruges, 1st July, 1524.

Whom all things do tend, having a most lively example in her virtuous mother.

All the neighbour-kings and princes did greatly desire her for marriage. James the Fifth, King of Scots, after, Charles the Emperor, offering presently to give the possession of the whole Low-Countries ; then the French king for both his sons, first for the Dauphin, then for the Duke of Orleans; whom when King Henry did not accept, for their tender age, King Francis offered himself to marry her ; such was the fame of her virtue and worth, in which for particular reasons of state, none of them succeeded.

In King Edward's reign, when new Governors altered the religion, she could nor would not be persuaded by any entreaties or threats of the Protector, or any others, to shut her oratory or keep close her. chapel, which she had in her house, but openly to have Mass daily said, or suffer the least change in Catholic Religion. And when she saw the courses those new rulers took, in breaking her father's will, to which they were sworn before his death, she very courageously and roundly wrote to the Protector, admonishing him and the rest of the Council to look well what they did, not to abuse the king's minority in altering the laws,

will, and ordinances of his and her father King
Henry; for in doing so they might be called to
account about the same when the king her brother
should come to full years. And withal she told
them plainly, that they had no authority to make
such alteration in so great matters as they did;
but rather to conserve things in the state left
unto them by the king her father, according to
the solemn oath they had sworn unto him before
his death, that they would do so, especially about
matters of Religion, until the king her brother
came to lawful age. And when they did not dare
publicly to persecute her, being the next to the
crown, they took from her her chaplains, punished them for not obeying the laws enacted; whereof she complained to her brother and wrote to
the Emperor how they dealt with her chaplains
and servants. Which the Emperor took hardly
that that could not be permitted to her, which
was to all ambassadors of foreign Princes; being
their king's elder sister, and professing the Catholic Religion in which she was bred and no other
known before those days in the kingdom of
England.

CHAPTER VI.

SKETCH OF THE REIGN OF QUEEN ELIZABETH.
CONTRAST BETWEEN HER AND QUEEN MARY.

I NOW pass to the education of Queen Elizabeth.
This would not be under her mother, for she was
not three years of age when her mother died.
She had been sworn princess of Wales a little
after her birth, and the Lady Mary deprived.
The king, shortly after her mother's death, in the
beginning of the month of June called an as-
sembly of the Bishops and a parliament, signify-
ing how much it did displease and repent him
of the wrong done his daughter Mary and the
advancing of Elizabeth, Anne Boleyn's daughter;
and would have it again as it was, and to con-
stitute some certain faith and form of religion.
For when Anne reigned all things were in
confusion, a licentious liberty was among all, nor
was it determined what they should believe or do
in matters of religion. For she (miserable woman)
was the first cause of the schism and bane of her

country. Yet she was a princess of majesty
and magnificence, and as one truly saith, fitter
for greatness than devotion and of more policy
than religion. Her sister Mary was no way
inferior as far as was fit for so great a princess,
only she was seventeen years older, but bred up
in all good learning, especially in virtue and
religion. Mr. Camden tells us that the Lady
Elizabeth read Melanchthon's Common Places; I
would she had in place thereof read St. Augustine's Meditations, Confessions and Soliloquies;
and for lives and living in matters of policy the
Saint's books *De Civitate Dei.*

A great lady, who knew her very well, being a
girl of twelve or thirteen, told me that she was
proud and disdainful, and related to me some
particulars of her scornful behaviour, which
much blemished the handsomeness and beauty
of her person. In King Edward's time what
passed between the Lord Admiral, Sir Thomas
Seymour, and her Dr. Latimer preached in a
sermon, and was a chief cause that the Parliament condemned tne Admiral. There was a bruit
of a child born and miserably destroyed, but
could not be discovered whose it was; only the
report of the midwife, who was brought from her

house blindfold thither, and so returned, saw nothing in the house while she was there, but candle light; only she said, it was the child of a very fair young lady. There was a muttering of the Admiral and this lady, who was then between fifteen and sixteen years of age. If it were so, it was the judgment of God upon the Admiral; and upon her, to make her ever after incapable of children. But the Admiral in September before had buried his wife, Queen Catharine, who died in childbed of a daughter. And it seems the cuckold then made no great reckoning of the Lady Elizabeth, for the great Lord Master was in 1550 created earl of Wiltshire, which was the title and honour of her father, transporting it from her and from his blood. And when after the death of King Edward they set up the Lady Jane they rejected her, fearing only Queen Mary. The reason why I write this is to answer the voice of my countrymen in so strangely exalting the Lady Elizabeth, and so basely depressing Queen Mary.

Queen Elizabeth's troubles began in the second year of her sister's reign. She was suspected and accused to be assistant unto the rebellion of Sir Thomas Wyatt, for which she was first committed to the Tower of London and afterwards re-

moved prisoner to Woodstock. Most of the
Council by the accusation of the delinquents and
other prescriptions would persuade the queen to
proceed against her by law; but her goodness
deferred it.

When Philip was come into England and
admitted king, finding the Lady Elizabeth to be
thus restrained, he dealt with the queen to be
merciful to her, and so delivered her not only
from extreme punishment but procured her
liberty to return to the Court. The remainder of
her sister's reign she lived for the most part in
her own house at Hatfield; to which place when
many suspected heretics and turbulent people
repaired, it seemed fit to the Privy Council that
the business should be no longer dissembled, but
questioned and punished. But the king and the
Spanish nobility favouring her, persuaded to
defer the matter. It broke out more manifest
the next year in March, when Sir Anthony
Kingston, Richard Udall, John Throckmorton,
John Daniel, William Stanton and others conspired together, not without counsel of the
French ambassador, to rob the king's treasure
which was provided for the French war. When
the matter was discovered by one of the con-

spirators, some were taken and executed, others fled into France. Hereof by many prescriptions was the Lady Elizabeth held accessory; which the queen's Council would have examined and chastised, but the king again protected her from this danger. It was consulted that two Catholic gentlemen should be sent to her to remain there and observe what passed, and so were sent Sir Thomas Pope and Mr. Robert Gage. But the lady by her wary carriage, her courteous behaviour and cunning, and by her public profession of Catholic religion with shew of zeal, did deceive these gentlemen. Before the year was ended, underhand she had intelligence with Mr. Thomas Stafford, who then exiled in France suddenly coming into England should title himself king, (for that he was descended from the house of the dukes of Buckingham) and should marry with the Lady Elizabeth; they supposing themselves strong enough against Queen Mary. It was not long before Mr. Stafford put this in execution; for coming out of France only with forty men on 24th April, 1557, and took Scarborough Castle, with hope that either the Lady Elizabeth would send her forces to fetch him, or with them to come to him herself. But when by the diligence of the

Earl of Westmoreland he was intercepted, sent
to London and beheaded, and some others of his
faction hanged, the relics of this crime remained
upon the Lady Elizabeth. It was her luck that
at this time King Philip had returned from
Flanders into England, by whose singular favour
she again escaped this plunge.

Queen Mary in her last sickness sent Com-
·missioners to examine her about religion, to
whom she answered, " Is it not possible that the
queen will be persuaded I am a Catholic, having
so often protested it ? " and thereupon did swear
and vow that she was a Catholic. This is
answerable to what Mr. Camden saith, and is
likewise confirmed by the Duke of Feria's letter
to the king, who in this sickness of the queen
visited the Lady Elizabeth. He certified him
that she did profess the Catholic religion and
believed the Real Presence, and was not like to
make any alteration for the principal points of
religion.

Queen Mary's reign began 6th July, 1553. She
returned all things that concerned the state of
religion as her grandfather, King Henry VII.,
had left them, and as they had been continued
by all Christian princes from the time when the

Christian religion entered into England. She abrogated all statutes of innovations and new devices during the time of her brother and father, reducing all to the humble obedience of the faith. She punished divers of the heads of those innovations that had been made; and above others, the chief author of all, Thomas Cranmer, who entering as a Catholic, as was supposed, into that dignity, was the first archbishop that ever failed in faith from the rest that were before him and from the obedience of the See Apostolic. This queen forgave the subsidies granted in the last year of her brother, gave great alms to the poor, remitted the debts of such officers of her house as she found burthened, restored more noble houses decayed than ever did prince in England, and brought with her peace and plenty. In a word, for magnaminity and virtue she was the worthiest princess that this kingdom ever had; and yet heresy had so enchanted the minds of divers of her subjects as in the five years of her reign she had more open and violent oppositions of her own subjects than Queen Elizabeth had in the forty-five years almost that she reigned.

Plain was the government of this queen, without tricks or new devices, severe to foul sinners

against God and sharp to such as offended
against the crown, to which she was more forced
than by nature inclined. She was a great
justicier, yet withal how merciful she was
appeared manifestly by her gracious compassion
to the Duchess of Somerset, to Sir John Cheke,
Sir Edward Montague, Chief Justice, Sir John
Cholmeley, the Marquis of Northampton, Sir
Henry Dudley, Sir Francis Gates, the Lord
Robert Dudley, and to the Duke of Suffolk;—all
of them her professed enemies and most of them
attainted, all adverse to her religion and no
friends to her title; and yet she released them all
out of the Tower, where they were prisoners.

Yet the Protestants were still busy against her
and gave her no quietness. They libelled against
the Government of Woman, published discourses
and invectives against religion, and conspired her
deprivation to advance her successor. All these
sedicious actions had for their ground the religion
then not fully six years old; a religion of mere
liberty, most pleasing to gallants, void of all
austerities. They cried her down because so
many were burnt in her time; but she caused no
new laws to be made against heretics but only
recalled such as were used and of force in God's

Church since the Christian religion was established in England. And when in any did concur
the faults of heresy and treason, or felony, her
will was that the law should proceed, heresy
being directly offensive and immediately against
God.

Queen Mary having lived thirty-seven years a
maid, for the good of her country, to leave issue
married the noblest prince of Christendom, who
brought wealth, honour, and the best alliance in
Europe to the crown of England. Yet see what
treasons and conspiracies did follow. Sir Thomas
Wyat's rebellion in the east of England; Sir
Peter Carew, Sir Gawen Carew and Sir Thomas
Dennie in the west; Sir James Croftes and others
in Wales; the Duke of Suffolk (after he had
been pardoned) in Leicestershire. Then, after
that, the conspiracies of the Earl of Devonshire,
Sir Nicholas Throckmorton and others. And
William Thomas, who plotted to murder the
queen, being a secretary in King Edward's time;
who, when he was executed said he died for his
country. After this were Udall, Throckmorton
and others, with Thomas Stratford, of whom I
have touched before.

Queen Elizabeth succeeded in the kingdom on

17 November, 1558, king Philip being in France
before Dourleus. She was persuaded by her new
councillors to resume the spiritual power and
jurisdiction. And it is probable that she was
persuaded, seeing what she had vowed in the
sickness of Queen Mary to the Commissioners
that examined her, and what she told the Duke
of Feria, and what she protested to ambassadors
and divers others at several times often, as is
noted by Catholic writers, who related divers
particulars, as that she showed devotion to the
Holy Cross, to our Blessed Lady and to the
Saints. When she died she had next her body
a crucifix of gold, hanging before her breast, so
that Doctor Barlow said she died a Papist. Yet
it seems that these men who would erect a new
religion followed their own persuasions, and by
little and little turned all upside down ; and by
them she was drawn to make such grievous laws
against Catholics as never prince before her did
make against any malefactor whatsoever. And
this is witnessed by the multiplicity of statutes
yet extant, the death of so many priests and the
affliction of innumerable subjects for that cause.

The queen before her Coronation put all
bishops to silence and commanded they should

not preach; and after the Parliament all that refused the oath were deprived of honours, livings and employments, either in Church or Commonwealth, and were committed to prison. There were in all of England fourteen bishops, most learned prelates, ten of Ireland, deposed; twelve deans, fifteen masters of colleges, six abbots, twelve archdeacons, one hundred and sixty priests, and Mr. Shellie, Prior of St. John's of Jerusalem.

The Communion Book, which was their new Church Service Book, was composed by Parker, Grindall, Horne, Whitehead, Bill, and Sir Thomas Smith. Was it ever known in a Christian kingdom that a course for religion was devised and framed without the consent and assistance of a bishop? But this was now done by these new upstarts and laymen, who afterwards made themselves bishops. In the disputations that followed the president appointed was Sir Nicholas Bacon, a mere layman, then made Lord Keeper. He being a great lawyer, but no divine, was one of the chiefest of them that persuaded the queen to take the course she did and to alter religion.

The end of the good bishops was this. Dr.

Scott, Bishop of Chester, died at Louvain in exile; Goldwell of St. Asaph at Rome; Pate of Worcester subscribed at the Council of Trent for the clergy of England, and never returned; Dr. Oglethorp of Carlisle, who consecrated the queen, died suddenly and shortly after his deprivation; learned and famous Tunstall died a prisoner at Lambeth; Bourne of Wells was prisoner to Carew, dean of the chapel; Thirlby of Ely was committed to the Tower and afterwards to Lambeth, where he died; Abbot Fecknam, Bishop Watson, Bishop White and Bishop Bonner died prisoners; and Prior Shelly in exile. This was the downfall of the Catholic clergy, a thing incredible to posterity.

The queen when she came to the crown was full twenty-five years of age, a gracious lady and gallant of aspect. Yet she would not be persuaded to marry, but would have it written on her tomb that she lived and died a virgin. King Henry the Fourth of France merrily said that the world would never believe this, nor would the many favourites she had, as Pickering, before she was queen, so as the world thought he should have married her. Nor would Leicester, nor Packington, nor Hatton, nor Rawley, nor Essex. To write all that might be said of her would fill many volumes. Mr. Camden in his Annals of her life has done it very partially, in many passages not telling all he ought to have done, and aggravating some passages, especially of Catholics. His conscience might tell him that all was not performed that he promised in his Epistle; and particularly in the relation of the proceedings, condemnation and death of the Queen of Scots, his majesty's mother, and the nearest kinswoman in blood the queen had, whose death was an eternal brand to our Queen Elizabeth. Yet her happiness is highly extolled by flattering heretics and such as know not, or will not know what passed before her reign, in her reign, and in her death. There was the ruin of many in her brother's and sister's time for her cause, the great distractions of her subjects' minds through the multitude of sects and differences in religion; the abundance of bloodshed of Catholic priests, honest men and of known integrity; the continual oppression of her subjects with subsidies and taxes; her assistance to other rebels against their natural princes, as the Hollanders and the Huguenots. There was that unjust law of the Supremacy to be

H

ministered to the people, the refusal of which by
them was treason, but not to be ministered to
the nobility. Also her injuries done to the King
of Spain in taking his treasure, in permitting
some of her nobility to be commanders in matters
of piracy and robbery; permitting Drake and
others to rob his ships, spoil his towns, and
capture his people, she herself first giving cause
of hostility; thus much annoying him who was
three times the cause of saving her life and
redeeming her liberty.

But now to come to her death. It grew of a
strange melancholy, very likely reflecting upon
the rehearsed particulars. Now that she had
grown old her beauty was much decayed. She
suspected that some of the greatest about her
looked towards Scotland. These considerations
took from her all magnanimity. Her negligence
in serving Almighty God suffered her to fall into
a distracted sadness and deep melancholy before
she died. For before she fell very sick, being at
Whitehall her senses, appetite and rest decayed,
and she was troubled with fearful visions;
whereupon she removed to Richmond and fell
sick indeed. She told a lady, one of the nearest
about her person, that she had seen a bright

flame about her, and asked her if she had not seen visions in the night. Growing more sick, she, all dressed, sat two days and three nights in her chair, and would be persuaded by none to go to her bed, or eat, or drink. Only the Lord Admiral persuaded her once to drink some broth, for to no other would she answer a word; but she said softly to him if he had known what she had seen in her bed he would not persuade her as he did. Commanding the rest of the lords to depart her chamber she willed the Lord Admiral to stay, to whom she shook her head and with a pitiful voice said to him " My Lord, I am tied with a chain of iron about my neck." He alleging her wonted courage she replied ; " I am tied, and the case is altered with me."

There was discovered in the bottom of the queen's chair a card (the Queen of Hearts) with an iron nail knocked through the head of it, which the ladies durst not then pull out, thinking it to be some witchcraft. So the queen, growing past recovery, kept her bed some days. The Archbishop of Canterbury and some other prelates were sent to her, but she was much offended on seeing them ; she cholericly rated them, and bid them be packing. Afterwards she exclaimed to the Lord Admiral that she had the greatest indignity offered to her by the archbishop that a prince could have, to pronounce sentence of death against her as if she had lived an atheist. And some lords offering to send some other prelates to her, she answered that she would have none of those hedge-priests. So none came to her until she was past sense and at the last gasp, when they said some prayers not far from her. Thus ended that great queen after forty-four years, four months and a few days' reign in great worldly glory and pleasure. It is not known that in all this sickness she said "God help me!" or any prayer or aspiration calling on God or asking His mercy.

But now it is time, after this long digression, to return to our lady duchess.

CHAPTER VII.

THE ARRIVAL IN ENGLAND OF THE DUKE OF
FERIA. HIS HISTORY AND CHARACTER. HE
MARRIES JANE DORMER.

WHEN King Philip, the Prince of Spain, came
into England to marry the queen, many great
personages and noble gentlemen did attend him,
among whom was El Conde Don Gomez de
Figueroa y Cordova, afterwards Duke of Feria, a
great Lord and Grandee of Spain, much favoured
by him and of his Council of State. This man began to look with particular affection upon the
duchess, curious (as the Spaniard is) to know her
birth, descent and quality. He finding both in
antiquity and other titles of honour not to be
inferior to his (although great men of Spain seldom marry out of their own rank and nation),
intended to solicit a match, moved thereto by the
favour she had with the queen, and the grace and
beauty of her person. And this affection, as much

grounded upon her virtuous parts as on the rareness of her beauty (the duke was then thirty-eight years of age), considering all the parts of this fair lady, esteemed him happy who should enjoy her. Which is an apparent argument of the worth, gentle and modest behaviour of the duchess, that not only the greatest of her own country, but of foreign nations did pretend her. And seeing it was the happiness of a stranger to obtain this pretence, he had the more obligation to esteem her, leaving country and friends and as good matches for his sake, which, as I noted before, the duke himself attested in his last will and testament. For which last will, having beseeched the king to be pleased that the duchess, the Lady Jane Dormer, his dear, most beloved and lawful wife, might choose two towns of his estate, with their jurisdictions, civil and criminal, and their whole rents and profits, wherewith she might entertain herself for the time that she should live. "And this, I am obliged" (saith he) "to ask of your majesty, because the duchess hath left the principal matches of her country and trusted in me a stranger, her servant and vassal." These are the words of the duke in his last testament. In this election of a husband, as in the course

and proceedings of her life, she imitated the virtue and prudence of the queen her mistress. For
when the queen, by the humble supplication of
the whole kingdom, and by the judgment and
advice of her wise and Catholic Council, intend-
ing to that which was most convenient for the
public good, determined to marry ; judging thereby, all matters as well for Religion as government might be better established by hopeful
succession. And albeit, divers were propounded
both within and without the kingdom, yet at last
the resolution was to have the marriage with
the Prince Philip of Spain, son to the Emperor
Charles V. as most honourable and beneficial to
the kingdom. So also the duchess preferred
before great lords at home, this noble stranger of
Spain, the duke of Feria. The king and queen
gave their willing consent for this marriage ; but
she would in no case have it solemnized until the
king's return from Flanders, whither the king
went about the wars which were made upon the
frontiers of France, and with him went the duke.

In the meantime the Queen fell sick, whereof
she died, to whom the king sent the duke to visit
her, but the king returned not. After the death
of the queen, and her funeral accomplished, the

duchess retired to her grandmother, who then lay at her house in the Savoy,[1] where the duke, prosecuting the desire of the marriage to be affected, it was solemnized in the church of the Savoy the 29th of December, being the feast of the renowned martyr St. Thomas of Canterbury. Although very unwilling, her uncles, the Earl of Sussex and Sir Henry Sidney, did agree to this marriage; being distasteful to them to see such their niece of that esteem and regard to leave country, kin, and friends to go to live with a stranger in a country so far from them, and in a climate so different from theirs. But Almighty God had so ordained it, and the duke held it his happiness to be her husband, whom for her virtue and worth he prized, as he said, beyond all the states and professions of the world.

[1] The palace of the Savoy, the residence of the dukes of Lancaster, was wrecked by the mob in their hatred of John of Gaunt in 1381. It lay in ruins until Henry VII. by his last will gave it as an hospital for a master and four chaplains. Suppressed by Edward VI., it was revived by Queen Mary. Having a considerable portion of the building to spare, the Master seems to have been in the habit of letting it out as lodgings. The account of Dr. George Montague, in 1608, contains an entry which shews that Sir Robert Dormer then occupied the lodging formerly occupied by his grandmother. The early registers having been destroyed by a fire, no record of the marriage of the duke is to be found. See Newcourt, 1—696.

The duke was yet resident as ambassador and vicegerent of his king; and held his authority with great valour and wisdom; and showed great zeal and devotion to Catholic Religion. For when the new queen began to alter and pervert the sacred office of the Church, to annihilate the ancient laws that touched Religion, which her deceased sister had renewed, the day that she should be crowned, the duke being earnestly requested from the queen and importuned by the Council to be present at her coronation (as he had been present when she rode through London and was installed queen,) he demanded, if in the coronation there would be performed all the usual ceremonies that were observed in the coronation of other Christian kings, according to the Catholic Church and ancient use of Catholic princes in this kingdom. And perceiving by their answer, there would be some alteration, he by no means would be entreated to assist there, neither publicly in the Church, nor in secret apart, or in a place that should be provided for him; for that he would not authorize by his presence any act that gave not due observation to the honour and custom of the Catholic Church.

About that time came into England, for

Leger-Ambassador the Bishop of Aquila.[2] The king, still remaining in Flanders, sent for the Duke of Feria, who, before his departure out of England, at the motion and instance of the duchess his wife, by way of petition asked of the queen to do him the favour to give him the Religious, both men and women, of her kingdom that would go with him; for that he would procure to dispose them to such parts where they might freely serve God and keep the rules of their profession. He had before this tried all possible ways to persuade the queen and her new councillors not to change nor alter the Catholic Religion which she found publicly professed when she succeeded in the crown, but would permit the laws established for it to stand in force; promising by the power and assistance of the king to clear all difficulties and resist all oppositions. But all in vain, for what smooth answers they gave they put in practice the contrary. What he requested touching the Religious to go out of England, he obtained, although with grief and trouble of some of the

---

[2] Alvaro de Quadra, Bishop of Aquila, of whom many notices occur in the Foreign Correspondence of the early years of Queen Elizabeth.

principal councillors, who murmured and put in many stumbling-blocks to hinder it, alleging to the queen many inconveniences that might grow to herself and her proceedings by this permission. Notwithstanding the duke desisted not (such was his courage and zeal) pressing the queen with her word and promise, but got as many of them together as he could and would come to Durham house where he lodged, and there he sustained them until he procured their passage for Flanders. In which company were three convents; one of the Carthusian monks of Sheene,[3] who by the Providence of God remain yet an entire convent, at Mechlin in Brabant; another of nuns of the holy order of St. Bridget who were of Sion,[4] which monastery also yet remains whole, of many noble gentlewomen and blessed sisters at

[3] They had been reinstated in 1556. Twelve professed monks and three lay brothers, with their prior, Maurice Chauncey, left England and arrived in Flanders 1st July, 1559. They resided successively at Bruges, Louvain, Mechlin and Nieuport until their final dissolution by the Emperor Joseph II. in 1783.

[4] The MS. history of this convent, formerly belonging to the Earl of Shrewsbury states that "By means of the Duke of Feria the nuns obtained licence of the queen to depart in the first year of her reign, the said duke preparing a ship by order of King Philip for their secure passing the seas."

Lisbon in Portugal; a third was of St. Dominic's
Order of the nuns of Dartford; [5] but being few,
they were soon dispersed in monasteries of their
own order. And when the duke went out of
England, which was about the end of May, 1559,
he had with him many priests, as afterwards in
the train of the duchess followed many others.
And being arrived where the king was he presented to his majesty their case, beseeching his
favour and protection; which the king promised
with great charity and piety, as became so great
and Catholic a prince.

The duke left the duchess at his house in
London, where she remained almost to the end
of July; at which time Don Juan de Ayala,[6] sent
by the king and duke for her, came to London.
The duchess was presently to put herself in order
for the voyage; and on the 24th of July she went
to take the leave of Queen Elizabeth; and
expecting in the presence-chamber, until the

---

[5] See on the history of this foundation Tanner's Not. Monast.
p. 225.

[6] The credence given to John de Ayala on being sent to
Queen Elizabeth in order to conduct the Countess of Feria
into Flanders, is dated at Ghent, 9th July, 1559. See Calend.
of Foreign Papers, No. 959. The queen's reply to Philip's
letter is dated on the 25th of the same month. Id. No. 1060.

queen called for her, and staying long, the
Spanish Ambassador began to be angry, desiring
her either to sit down or to return, for she was
now seven months gone with child. The bishop
spake loud, seeing who she was and with child,
that it was not fit she should stand there waiting,
and would have pressed her to sit down in the
chair of State. Which when the queen understood she presently came forth.[7] That compli-
ment done, within two days following she took
her journey towards Dover, where she was to be
embarked. She went accompanied with a troop
of noble gentlemen and ladies, her kin and friends,
among whom was the Lord Bishop, Leger-
Ambassador, who had special commandment
from the king to have care of her. Also went
with her the good lady, her dear and beloved
grandmother, taking that opportunity to go where
she might freely and securely serve God and

---

[7] A version of this story, intended for the guidance of Sir
Thomas Challoner, the English ambassador at Madrid, was
sent to him by Cecil in a letter dated 27th July. Of course it
exonerates Elizabeth and places the conduct of the Bishop of
Aquila in the most unfavourable light. Cecil speaks with
respect of the Countess of Feria. See Foreign Papers of
Elizabeth, 27th July, 1559, No. 1082. The farewell interview
took place on the 23rd July.

enjoy the help and means for it. The duchess
had attending on her six gentlewomen, the
daughters of noble and principal gentlemen.
One was sister to the Lord Harrington, her
cousin-german; another sister to Sir Edward
Stradling; another sister to Sir William Pickering, the queen's favourite; another was Mrs.
Paston, who afterwards returning to England,
was married to Sir Henry Newton of Gloucester-
shire, and became of the bed-chamber to Queen
Elizabeth, and others; and with these Mrs.
Clarentia, who from the childhood of Queen Mary
had served her, and ever in principal place about
her; a woman respected and beloved by the queen,
who the rest of her life remained with the
duchess. Besides the priests that were permitted
to go over, divers gentlemen sheltered themselves
under her protection, to go where they might
according to their desire serve God.

Arrived at Dover, after taking leave of friends,
where was the Earl of Sussex and Sir Henry
Sidney, the next day after dinner she embarked
for Calais, where within few hours she landed,
received by Monsr. Gourden, governor of Calais,
whither came also the governor of Boulogne to
visit her. And after a day's rest and two nights,

having been very honourably entreated and feasted by those governors in the town of Calais, she took her journey for Graveling, thence for Dunkirk, places subject to the King of Spain; in both which she was received with extraordinary great feasts and triumphs, discharging all the artillery of the place. The governors meeting her with their captains and soldiers marching in military order, giving all signs of welcome entertainment, presenting her with gifts accustomed in such places to noble personages.

From Dunkirk she passed Newport and came to Bruges,[8] where she rested some days; whither came the duke her husband to receive her and Don Luys Mendes, sent by the king to visit her and bid her welcome into those parts. Also thither came Don Antonio de Toledo, brother to the Duke of Alva, Commander of the Order of St. John and Grand-Prior of Castille. In this city (as in the rest), the magistrates and governors of the places adjoining did her great honour by their rich presents, and gave testimony of their

[8] Writing to Cecil on July 29th, Challoner reports that the Countess of Feria had been princely met upon the way, and would rest her in a Spaniard's house at Bruges. Foreign Papers of Elizabeth, No. 1093.

the Cardinal Granville and the Bishop of Tour-
nay; the godmothers were the Duchess of
Parma,[12] governess, and the Countess of Hoch-
straete,[13] (for the use then was there to have two
godfathers and two godmothers) which was performed in most honourable and princely manner.

When the child was borne to the church, first
were divers noble personages carrying such things
as are used in baptism, the candles, the basin
and ewer, the salt, the chrism, etc. Then
followed the eldest daughter of the countess-
godmother, who did bear the child, and the
younger daughter, both gorgeously apparalled,
who carried the train of the child's mantle.
Then next followed Madam Governess, and next
to her the other godmother, attended with all the
ladies and nobility of the Court. The child was
christened by the name of Laurence, the name
of his grandfather, Count of Feria and Marquis
of Pliego; it being the custom that the heirs of
this house retain, *alternis vicibus*, the names of
Gomez and Laurence for many ages.

[12] Margaret, wife of Alexander de Medicis, Duke of Florence,
and subsequently of Octavian Farnese, Duke of Parma.

[13] Apparently Anne de Rennenberg, wife of Philip de Lalaing,
who died 14th August, 1555. See Théatre Profane de Brabant,
II, 39.

CHAPTER VIII.

THE JOURNEY OF THE DUCHESS INTO SPAIN.
HER MARRIED LIFE. BIRTH OF HER SON
AND DEATH OF HER HUSBAND.

WHEN the solemnity of the christening was ended the duchess, for to recover strength, remained
at Mechlin to the beginning of March following.
Her grandmother then parted from her to settle
herself in Louvain, as hath been said. The duke
took of an Italian merchant in Antwerp fifty
thousand ducats, which he borrowed for the journey into Spain for himself, the duchess and the
child, then six months old. The duchess went
first to Brussels, where she was entertained with
extraordinary signs of congratulation, as in other
places where she entered. There she stayed until the first of April, A.D. 1560, on which day
(being the Monday before Palm Sunday) she, her
husband and the infant Marquis her son, began
their journey towards Spain, accompanied with
many noble gentlemen and their attendants,

among whom was Sir William Shelley, of the
Order of St. John, Grand Prior of England.
They had for their better commodity double provision; to wit, that the furniture which served
this day was carried before to serve the second
day following, so as their servants had all things
beforehand, where they should lodge, in readiness.

When they came to the frontiers of France
many noble personages came to receive them,
and Mons. D'Oussons was sent by the king and
queen to welcome them into the country and to
conduct them to the court.   And in every town
where they lodged the keys were brought to the
duke, to be master of them that night.   Coming
to St. Denis in the Holy Week they rested there until Easter Eve.   That day, in the afternoon, they
entered into Paris and were lodged in the Duke of
Guise's house, who was the queen's uncle, where
they remained the Easter holidays and were
visited by many.   After that they went on their
journey towards Amboise, where the king and the
queen regent and the queen's mother lay; the
king then being Francis the Second, son of Henry
the Second, and this queen was Queen Mary of
Scotland, mother of King James, now king of
Great Britain.

They being arrived at the court, the princes sent to welcome them, and the queen commanded to bring the duchess to her palace, having ordered to provide a lodging for her. No sooner was the duchess entered into the palace but the Queen Regent came presently to visit her, who beholding her beauty, the sweetness of her countenance and the good grace of her person—they are the queen's own words, which I have heard from her secretary and a gentlewoman, his sister, one of the two that were admitted to be present at her death, —who heard the queen divers times report it, was marvellously taken with her presence, and showed affection for her; as when wearing mourning for the death of the king, her father-in-law, she that day put it off, to honour the duchess, and clothed herself in white. She also entreated the duchess that she also would be apparelled after the French manner, which, to please the queen, she yielded to: and the queen would have her clothed in her presence, which her Majesty did put her hand to, taking in it very particular content, for she would mend what the women had done; and from that time the queen began to bear her so entire and intimate love as she continued to keep it to her death, with many remonstrances.

That day she was invited to eat at the queen's table, who commanded the guard of the Scots gentlemen to wait on her, and did her so many royal courtesies as she would have done to any strange princess that had been nearest of her blood. She brought her to the queen's mother, who very kindly treated her, and promised afterwards to visit her herself. At her departure she sent divers to accompany her to the borders of Spain, and required with great charge, as occasions fell out, that she might hear from her and she would not fail to answer her; yea, and to provoke her to write to her. This correspondence continued while they lived, the queen subsigning all her letters, "Your perfect friend, old acquaintance and dear cousin, Maria Regina." Divers of which letters I have seen, and have four or five of them by me, written all with the queen's own hand, very affectionate and respectful. This respect was evidently to be seen when the duke her husband died, the queen being then detained prisoner in England, in the year 1571. She desired that the duchess might come into Flanders; and wrote unto his Catholic Majesty beseeching him that it might be so with his license, for that the duchess living in Flanders would be much for the service of God's.

Church and of her Majesty, and that she should
so enjoy better health, being a climate more
agreeable to her natural constitution than that
of Spain; and that the queen for her part
should receive great consolation to have her so
near herself, and in regard of her present afflictions she should reap thereby both comfort and
benefit. And to this end did her Majesty also
write to his Holiness, commanding his ambassador
to solicit it very seriously as a matter very convenient to his service and her solace ; and likewise to deal with the Ministers of his Catholic
Majesty, that the journey of the duchess to
Flanders might take effect. This the Queen of
Scotland desired exceedingly to accomplish, as
her secretary,[1] who wrote these letters, hath related
to me, a man very prudent and Christian, who
lived and died a very virtuous and pious Catholic;
for I am witness to both, having familiarly been
acquainted with him for almost six years, and by
him daily in his last sickness and present at his
death ; a little before which, calling Father Creswell and the gentlemen and men of any fashion,

[1] A marginal note in the MS. tells us that this was " Monsr.
Gilbert Curle, secretary more than twenty years to the Queen
of Scots."

both English and Scots, he there protested upon
hope of his salvation, of his fidelity and true loyal-
ty ever to the queen, his mistress, both living
and dead, against the calumnies and imputations
put in print, the authors being too lightly credulous.
And this he spake (myself being a witness) with
great asservation, protesting his innocence ever
at the last gasp as he should answer it before the
tribunal of the Eternal Judge. This I hold myself bound in conscience to write ; for that he desired all the assistants to witness what he affirmed
upon his death-bed. The queen spake often of
the duchess, uttering words of great affection, much
commending her virtue and worth. But this
desired journey could not take effect by reason of
the minority of her son.

But to proceed with the duchess' journey.
They arrived in Spain with good health, and
about the end of June came to Segovia, the king
and queen being then at a house of recreation in
the woods adjoining; but the court then resided
in Toledo, to which place was referred the
journey of the duchess for their majesties. Into
which city she entered the 9th of August, the
vigil of St. Laurence, 1560, with that honourable
lustre and unusual greatness that the houses of

the whole city were dispeopled to behold her entrance. The king and the duke her husband stood together in a window to see her pass, she riding on horseback; the furniture of her horse being of crimson velvet garnished with studs and fringe of gold, and another horse led by, very richly appointed. Her six dames likewise were all alone on horseback, with velvet furniture, suitable alike. The duchess had attending on her twenty pages, all in costly liveries, and was accompanied with most of the gallantry of the court. But her own person graced all. The king, before she visited the queen, came himself to see her, to bid her welcome to the court of Spain.

The next day she went to kiss the queen's hands, who was the eldest daughter of France;[2] and so could give her account of the queen her mother, the king her brother, his queen and the other princes, her brothers and sisters; in whose court she had been so honourably entertained. The queen received her with much shew of kindness and favour, as much admiring her beauty as envying her nation; and she gave her a jewel for her welcome. The king of Portugal[3] sent of

---

[2] Isabella, daughter of Henry II., King of France.
[3] Sebastian, King of Portugal, from 1557 to 1578.

purpose to visit her, and to give her the Bienvenida into those countries, and withal a fair jewel for a present, which I have seen; and it was valued by the jeweller at 8,000 ducats. For some days these visits of welcome continued. The respect of the duke her husband, the report of her virtue and the comeliness of her presence drew a regard and honour to her of the whole court, by all performances, in such noble and extraordinary manner as the memory thereof remains much extolled, especially among the kindred, allies and vassals of that house of Feria and Cordova.

After that the duchess had rested in the Court she repaired to Zafra, the duke's house on his own estate in Estramadura, where she was received by the neighbouring gentlemen and tenants with such tokens of honour as could not be greater nor more costly. Here now she begins to put in practice the state of a married wife. And although by the means of heats of that country, so different from this where she was born and brought up, she had so little health as she was in a sort unfit to intend to anything besides her prayers and her health; yet now being in her own house she resembles her grandmother, of whom she would be a perfect follower, seeking to treasure up in herself the degrees and excellencies of a good and perfect wife; so that her husband found in her a general treasure for all cares and chances. In all times and all occasions she sought to please him and increase his contentment. For in mirth, the duchess was to him sweet and pleasing company; in matters of discontentment he found in her a lively comfort; in doubts a faithful and able counsellor; in adverse accidents a solace. All that knew them, knew how much the duke esteemed her, how dearly he loved her; for all those qualities he acknowledged to be in the duchess, as such as served them (and not in mean place) have attested to me with particular relation.

But for more complete testimony hereof is his last will and testament, wherein he distinctly remembereth those great parts in her, leaving her the only tutoress of their son and the governess of his estate, until the time by the law made he was capable thereof, which is at twenty-five years of age; he being not full twelve years when his father died. For among other words in his testament of her praise, he hath these; " I beseech of the duchess no particulars,—for that I

know what belongeth to the bringing up of her
son and the government of his lands, goods and
house, she will do much better than I do know to
ask it, etc." Withal charging his son, upon his
blessing and under pain of his curse, to love and
obey her; and telling him the great obligation she
had to her more than to a mother. As she was
to her husband, a respecting, loving and provident wife; so to her son she was a careful
mother, notable instructor, and a most prudent
tutoress. Her care gave him those principles
and foundations of wisdom, virtue and excellence,
wherewith he so shined and flourished in the
world as is singularly expressed in the funeral
oration at the solemnity of his funeral at Zafra.
Her prudent education instilled in him the
beginning and entrance to know how to govern
himself and others; for when upon the death of
his father, the king gave him the Encomienda [4]
of Segura de la Sierra, one of the richest in
Spain, which his father had before him, when he
had taken the habit of Santiago, she caused him
to go to the monastery of Santiago at Urles,
according to the custom of the Order, and would
not take dispensation for him, as others of his

[4] A grant or benefice attached to a military order.

quality do, but that he being young should perform his noviceship; which he did some months in serving Mass and performing other duties that he might the better know his obligations to God's service; at times, taking the recreations of so great a person. This education brought him to the fame and deserved renown he had in the world.

She was in her family a lady that gave remedy to their wants; cause of exercise and employment both to menservants and women according to their quality, detesting idleness, being herself a rare example of industry, piety, and imitable government.

About five years after her marriage she had another son, whom in baptism they called Don Pedro, after his great-grandfather by the grandmother's side. But this child had not accomplished three months when it pleased God to take him again.

It would ask a large discourse to relate the many memorable acts of the Christian zeal of this duchess while she was a married wife; but I will content myself in proof and testimony hereof to repeat what a great author doth affirm and hath published in print.

Fra Juan Baptista Moles, a Recollect Des-
calced of the Order of St. Francis, in his
Memorial that he wrote of the same province,
observes as followeth:[5] "The said Dukes of
Feria are, and have always been, patrons of this
house, who ordinarily repair hither and supply
with liberal hand the necessary occasions of the
same, accounting this house for their particular
recreation, in which they have a lodging (which
I have seen) where commonly, when they reside
in *Zafra*, they retire themselves in Lent, and for
the Holy Week, and other principal feasts of the
year. With the most singular devotion this did
the great duke, Don Gomez, first Duke of Feria,
and the most Christian duchess his wife, the
Lady Jane Dormer, a marvellous devotee of our
habit and religion. They, recollecting themselves
in this house, did not only give to the religious
to eat; but on Holy Thursday and other special
days, they with their own hands did serve; giving
them their meat in the refectory, and imparting it
to them with so great humility and affection as if
they had done it to the Apostles of Jesus Christ.
Afterwards they themselves, eating with the
lay friars and treating them with great devotion

[5] Memorial de San Gabriel, cap. xlii.   Marg. Note in MS.

and plainness, left herein great edification to the religious, and a marvellous example for such like honourable persons. And so to this day liveth, and shall live for ever, the memory of this so pious and devout a lord among the religious, to commend his soul to God and to pray for the life of the duchess his wife, now a widow, who with great example and praise of her holy behaviour, continueth in the recollection of a very holy life; who having been visited by God with the loss of so worthy a husband, aparted from her country and nation; yet remaineth in solitariness, as she that is descended of noble and honourable blood in the kingdom of England; still having in remembrance this religious house de la Lapa; and providing for it and for the rest that are in her son's estate with such relief, alms and works of charity, as one very intimately devoted to this holy province and to the religious of the same."
This the said author, Fra Juan Baptista Moles, writeth in his said Memorial; and in another chapter following he saith further that the duke and duchess did found and build the monastery of our Lady de Monte-Virgine, situated half a league from the town of Villalva. And that after the duke's death his duchess, the Lady

being a stranger, young, out of her country, far from her friends, left in a manner wholly solitary, with the care and charge of the estate of the duchy in her only son, not yet twelve years of age.

Here might be amplified her attendance and diligence towards the duke in this sickness, the entire love and affection wherewith she served him, her great solicitude to regale him, to help him, to inquire after expert physicians and seek for remedies that might procure health; the continual labour she passed night and day, present at all hours to assist in what was needful, and to give contentment in all occasions. But human pains or diligence availed little either of wife or king (who sent of purpose to Guadaloupe for a physician) nor of kin nor of friends, nor of servants; for, all seeing and feeling their loss failed not to procure and do what they could for his health and recovery. The time was come that it pleased God that this good duke should leave this vale of misery, to live with the blessed Saints, there to receive the eternal reward of his merits, whereof living and dying he gave hopeful assurance by many evident and most Christian effects.

I might here declare the valour, wisdom and understanding and other excellent parts of this great duke, which were so notoriously apparent to the world where he lived; but I rather desire to pass them with silence, than by my inability not to give them their deserved right and honour; for with his death failed one of the noblest and best gentlemen that the kingdom of Spain had or knew in his time, or since then to this day, which is manifest by the many great and important affairs wherein from his youth he was employed both in peace and war. The regard that the Emperor Charles the Fifth had of him, commending him as a notable and able assistant to Philip his son, and the esteem and favour that he held with this king to his death, being of his Council of State, Captain of his Spanish Guard; called always by his majesty to his private consults and intimate conferences, which as a most noble true gentleman and worthy counsellor he applied not to his own interest, little respecting increase of his own lands and wealth, but the honour of his king, the service of his country, the benefit of the common-weal and the advancement of such as merited. Noble personages and honourable widows who were fallen into wants,

made suit to this good duke as their patron and
best advocate, and found help for their necessities.   Yea, it was very ordinary with him,
when strangers, were they English, Flemings,
or Italians, (especially if they were of quality,)
having suits and pretentions in the court, their
business requiring some time for examination,
(who often had much delay before they could be
despatched); this duke in the meantime gave
them allowance to sustain them; in so much
as when his steward made complaint that money
came not in to supply so much, and that he
wanted to provide what was necessary for his
own house; the duke would answer: "I have
plate, pawn it; and let not these men lack;"
compassionating their cases when their des-
patches were delayed.   He preferred the affairs
of the public weal before his own, were they
never so important.

The duchess herself told me, that the duke
and she talking in private and discoursing of the
sudden rising and great wealth of some that had
the king's ear and were in his favour; she object-
ing the little increase that the duke had made,
yet no man more in favour, no man more
constant, no man more intimate with the king

than he, seeing most businesses of estate were passed and despatched by his means ;—he answered : " Would you that I take gifts and bribes, or that my honour remain in the point it doth, and should ? For if I would accept presents and gifts, you must cause the back door to be opened to pass them out ; for your house would quickly be so full as it would not contain them. But to this day my honour hath not been touched with bribes, and shall I now begin ? " She replied : " If it concern your honour, in God's name let it be ; for to uphold your honour, I had rather be poor than give way to the least decay thereof."

He was affable and sweet in condition, not haughty, no despiser, not proud, used all with marvellous courtesy and a continuing liberality where there was need. The respect he had to ecclesiastical and religious persons was notable ; his zeal and fervour in observance of the Catholic Religion were admirable. He rather suffered the displeasure of his mother, whom he ever observed with all duty and obedient respect, and the hazard to lose that great estate of the marquis-ship of Pliego, whereof his mother was heir, than he would consent to marry the only daughter of his elder brother Don Pedro, who died young, leaving no other issue, being so near of his blood; whom his mother (otherwise a most virtuous lady) in revenge married to his younger brother and put the estate in process between the two brothers.

While his sickness lasted, which daily grew more dangerous by the violence of the fever, he disposed all matters as a Christian should do, confessed, received the Sacraments of the Holy Eucharist and Extreme Unction; had always about him religious men, spent the time as his sickness might permit, in spiritual discourses; comforting the duchess, setting before her eyes the will of Almighty God that all must obey; her own Christianity and discretion, and so to suffer with patience his departure, leaving as a pledge their son who should supply his place. And then he called his son and gave him his blessing; he charged him to serve God, to live virtuously, to honour and obey his mother, repeating to him the great duty he did owe her. He was very devout to our Blessed Lady; and so on the day of her birth, he was born to God.[1]

[1] Namely, on the festival of the Nativity of our Blessed Lady, 8th September, 1571.

The king felt his death so heavily as he shed tears; which is said he was never seen to do for any but for his son Don Carlos. But this heavy loss most touched the duchess in her particular, although it was general, both for the king's services, the benefit of his country, and for the causes and pretensions of the good and well-deserving, both subjects and strangers, religious and secular.

He was a great furtherer and advancer of the Fathers of the Society of Jesus (a Religion that hath merited so well by their great labours, learning, and good example, in the Church of God) as Father Ribadeneira in his Epistle (dedicated to the duchess) of his book *De los Santos Extravagantes*,[2] confesseth in these words: " It is long since that I have desired some good occasion to declare unto the world the obligations that all this little Society of Jesus hath to serve your excellency and your most honourable house; and I more than any, in regard I am so ancient a witness of the many and singular favours we have received from the hands of the most

---

[2] P. Ribadeneyra Epist. a Dona Juana Dormer, Duquesa de Feria, 15 de Julio 1608. See De Backer, Bibl. des ecrivains de la Compagnie de Jesus, iii. 154, ed. 1876.

excellent Lord Don Gomez de Figueroa y
Cordova, Duke of Feria,[8] your husband, and
which your excellency and the Duke Don
Lorenzo your son have always continued as true
lords, patrons, and defenders of our Society.
And for to say something of much that may be
said, in the year 1555 I went to Rome from
Flanders, sent by the blessed Father Ignatius,
our Father and Founder, for to be a suitor to his
Catholic Majesty to give us license to erect
colleges of the Society in those states, and there-
with to serve our Lord with our poor labours; as
by His grace, the Society doth in so many other
parts of the world. Which petition, although it
were very just, yet it had many and most sore
difficulties and contradictions of such persons
as had more obligation to favour and assist so
holy a work (as it falls out in the like for God's
service) which the Duke Don Gomez, by his
authority, valour, and wisdom, made plain and
obtained of the king all that I pretended. For,
as he was so great a lord, and so great a favourite
of his majesty, and brother to Father Antonio
de Cordova, who was of our Society, and son of
the most worthy Lady Donna Catalina Fer-

[8] See Hist. Societ. Jesu, by Orlandini, p. 402, ed. 1620.

nandez de Cordova, Marquesa de Pliego, and
brother of the Lady Donna Maria de Toledo,
Duchess of Arcos, who were notable protectors
of our Society and founders of the colleges of
Montilla and Marchena, his Excellency undertook
my protection ; and for the time that I remained
in that court he was my defence, advocate,
solicitor, powerful lord and loving father. He
effected that which seemed impossible, and
opened the door that stood so locked, that the
Society might have houses and colleges in all
those states. And by virtue of that license and
privilege, it hath at this day more than twenty,
and in them more than seven hundred persons in
the most principal cities and towns of the Low
Countries ; which much serve our Lord, illuminat-
ing and repressing heretics, animating Catholics,
and instructing them to live Christianly, to obey
God and their princes. And all this fruit, after our
Lord, Who would be served with it, the Society
oweth to the duke, as to the root from whence
it sprung."

And afterwards in the same Epistle he addeth
further, that in the year 1557 returning another
time from Rome to Flanders, " I received," saith
he, " many benefits and the whole Society in my

person.   And I went with his Excellency into
England in the year 1558, sent by the king to
assist in the infirmity of our lady and queen,
Queen Mary, etc."

Moreover, in the death of this duke, our country
and Catholics lost a main and evident hope of
their desire for the restitution of the Catholic
religion, knowing his zeal to further all means
and helps that might effect this restitution by
that which appeared he did in the beginning of
the change at his coming out of England; and
partly by undertaking the government of the
Low Countries, which was appointed to him in
the year 1571.   He provided for the journey;
but then his mortal sickness seizing upon him, it
pleased God to alter this expected happiness.   I
have been credibly informed that more than once
he hath with hearty instance insinuated to the
king that the relief of our country imported
much the reputation of his majesty; and that
before God and man he was bound in honour to
give remedy, seeing the ruin thereof came upon
his relinquishing it, his good queen and wife
having settled it in so good estate.   And that
his majesty could not forget what passed, he
being employed by him as his counsellor and

servant to preserve her that then stood and ruled; and contrary to hope and promise had confounded all. And that the duke had this zeal to our country appeareth by sundry letters written after his death in the Latin tongue to his majesty and to the duke, his son, wherein also appeareth the respect and esteem that the English Catholics had to the lady duchess, desiring that she might come into the Low Countries. This letter I found written with a most fair and legible hand, and subscribed with these names; namely, Doctors William Allen, Owen Lewis, Thomas Stapleton, Richard Hall, Richard White, William Carter, William Smith, William Knott, John Dauley, Licenciates, or Bachelors of Divinity; Henry Joliff, William Taylour, Thomas Wilson, Thomas Bailie, Laurence Webbe, Peter Foster, Cuthbert Vaux, Thomas Metham, Thomas Parker, Thomas Dorman, Giles Capell, Gregory Bell, Gilbert Branford, Edmund Hargatt, Thomas Hide, John Marshall, John Fenne, Thomas Freeman, Maurice Chancy, prior of the Carthusians, for him and his convent. This letter to his Catholic majesty was dated at Antwerp on 6th October, 1571.

A letter from the same writers to the Duke of

Feria on the death of his father was written on
the same day.

Another from the same to the Cardinal Protector was carried by Dr. Nicolas Sanders.

His Holiness Pope Pius Quintus did write
unto the duchess upon the news of the death of
the duke, which brief is dated at St. Peter's,
28th November, 1571, and subsigned, Ant.
Buccapedalius.

CHAPTER X.

OF THE WIDOWHOOD OF THE DUCHESS AND HER
VIRTUOUS EXERCISES IN THAT ESTATE.

THE duchess now in the eighteenth[1] year of her
marriage and thirty-fourth of her age, beset on
every side with the divers and heavy thoughts of
her widowhood, the present solitariness and the
heavy memory of her past contentment, yet so
moderated her passions (which commonly in
such accidents, even in the wisest, grow to

[1] Read, "the thirteenth." In the margin of the original
occurs this note,

"For the virtues of a widow read the fortieth chapter of
Francis of Sales, Bishop of Geneva, his *Introduction to a Devout
Life*, which our duchess practised before he wrote it."

extremes, affection over-ruling discretion, such is the force of these passions beyond reason) as considering all circumstances which I must repeat, yet so young, a stranger, so far from country and friends, her loss so important, must needs augment grief; and the more for that there was no remedy, for recovery; nevertheless, necessity did not persuade so much a moderation as religion directed to look upon her husband rather absent than dead; whereupon she resolveth a constant purpose to hold true fidelity to him and together to conform herself to the will and ordinance of God Almighty.

The duke in his death-bed recommended to this lady especially three things—his soul, his son, and his honour. His soul to be prayed for and assisted with the holy Sacrifice of the Church, alms-deeds and other good works of charity; his son to be brought up christianly, in the fear of God, learning and qualities answerable to his rank and condition; his honour to be taken care of, to pay his debts, and make satisfaction where it was due. Of all which she had so particular care as she neither slacked time, nor omitted opportunity with all speedy accomplishment to pay this performance as was requisite.

As concerning the first; presently upon his death, in all the monasteries and parishes about the Escurial and in Madrid, large alms was given to pray for his soul. And in the duke's estate, in many Religious houses, perpetual memories were founded to this end. And the duchess to her death did always continue the remembrance of this charge where she lived; and in her will, left particular charge, to the duke her grandson always to accomplish the aidful memory of his grandfather, father, and hers; observing with special solemnity his anniversary rites; which charge she commended to myself for divers years, to be done in most of the monasteries of Madrid with good alms.

For the second, which was the education of her son, is showed before in the description of his life and worthy parts.

And the third to uphold his honour in paying his debts and in giving satisfaction where aught might be with conscience required, and in maintaining the honourable estate of his house, she notably showed the effects of a loving wife and the affectionate memory of a most christian, industrious and provident lady. For at the death of the duke, his estate (for his own debts and the debts of the Count Don Pedro his elder brother, contracted for the service of their princes), stood engaged to the value of 300,000 ducats, which this good lady by her provident government in her time cleared. For when the duke her grandson entered into it, he found it free and discharged. He being employed to do the obedience to Pope Paul the Fifth, being the first employment and he young, would perform it with extraordinary greatness, and so put himself into a new engagement for that embassage, which was very little, considering how his grandmother found it when his grandfather died. This her government was not by withdrawing any allowance that touched the maintenance of her house or honour of her son ; or by new inventions or tricks to oppress her vassals or tenants, whom always she entreated with such sweetness and plausible proceedings as they extraordinarily respected, reverenced and affected her. Which to demonstrate, one example among many may make plain.

It happened in the year 1603 that the king made offer to farm out the tollage that was by Badajoz, upon the confines of Portugal. The duke, her son, was the viceroy of Sicily ; who, advertised of this farming, wrote presently to his

mother to take it for him, whatsoever it cost, because joining to his estate, it lay convenient for
him and more for him than any, and very prejudici-
ally and hurtful if any other should rent it. Which
the duchess receiving, presently sent to the king's
office accepting the farm, desiring to know the
price. It was replied forty thousand ducats; and
this same to be paid in few days all in ready
money; and to be paid as the order was before the
estate could be passed. The duchess put to this
exigence presently to provide so much money, living in Madrid, the Court being then at Valladolid
(almost one hundred miles off) where the money
was to be paid, by the assistance of a friend, she
presently had lent her fourteen thousand ducats.
For the rest, which was twenty-six thousand
ducats, she presently despatched a messenger,
writing to *Zafra* to the governor of the duke's
estate to call the tenants and solicit them for
this sum, showing the necessity of present payment, and promising by her letter repayment
within four months. The messenger came to *Zafra*
about eleven o'clock before noon. The governor having read the duchess her letter, sent his
man presently to most of the principal of the town
to meet him at the town-house at two o'clock;

in which place they assemble at the same hour.
The governor read to them the duchess's letter,
and so requested their answer. And this followed;
that by seven o'clock the same evening the whole
twenty-six thousand ducats were brought to the
governor's house without any further reply, or request of more security of bills or bands than the
promise of the bare letter that she wrote. This
the governor himself reported to me, admiring it
when we were at the solemnity of her funeral.
Such was the love and respect the tenants had
always to her, albeit a stranger; having merited
it by her affable and excellent government.

K

CHAPTER XI.

THE MODE OF LIFE OF THE DUCHESS DURING HER WIDOWHOOD.

THE duchess for her own private entertainment gave herself wholly from the death of her husband to a recollected kind of life, putting from her all ostentation of greatness, both in attendance, apparel, and house-furniture, as usually all widows of respect do in Spain. She, always upholding what was necessary for the service of her son and the managing of his estate, wholly employed her time in virtuous exercises, serving Almighty God in works of piety; wherein to her death she so exemplarly continued as that all sorts, both religious and secular, the greatest and the meanest, had her in respect and reverence.

So likewise was her house governed. Holiness at home; courage abroad; prudence everywhere. Her servants were provided of all things necessary according to their place, office, and merit; their rations and wages always paid most punctually. In sickness or other infirmities, her regard and severe commandment to have the physician called, were the sick man the meanest in her service; and orderly to be provided and given whatsoever the physician appointed. She gave leave and special charge to all her servants daily to hear Mass; and when Mass was read every day in her own oratory her care was that all her women servants should be present at the beginning; for the men-servants might go abroad to church. Very exact was her order that all her family should go to confession on all the solemn feasts of the year, and likewise the feasts of our Blessed Lady. That they should be advised to keep the Commandments of God and of His holy Church; should be friends of truth, extremely abhorring the contrary; should live in peace; be chaste and honest in their comport-ment; for the shew of the contrary in any gesture or condition did much offend her. Yea, she did so govern her house and family as she may be a notable example for others to follow. By her careful providence, disengaging her house, as hath been said, of such great debts as lay

upon it; and breeding up her son with that noble
and virtuous education, as hath been also declared. Her service was a school and pious
nursery of virtue and an exemplar to all that had
the happiness to serve her; for divers of them
left the world and became religious. I think
that during the forty years she lived a widow,
few passed that some or other went not out of
her house into religion, as I knew divers that
had been her servants of the Order of St. Francis,
both Descalços and others; some of St. Dominic's
Order, some Augustines, Benedictines, Jesuits, and
others. Thus was her house and family governed.

The second virtue of St. Paul's widow is, to
honour and have great respect to parents. According to the next and strict literal sense the
duchess had no matter to perform this counsel;
for that before she was a widow, her grandfather,
grandmother and mother died, and her father
soon after, who was in England married to
another wife and had divers children, and she in
Spain. But while he lived she was not unmindful
to offer and present the respect that did become
her; and for the deceased, her prayers and the
Sacrifice of the Church, which she had care
should be offered for their souls, were testimony

of her love and honour to them; giving large
alms to particular monasteries only for this
office. And the former course of her life (namely
to her grandmother who brought her up,) is a
plain evidence how mindful she was of this duty;
over whose body (which lieth in the choir before
the high altar in the Charterhouse of Louvain)
together with her sister, the Lady Hungerford,
she caused a fair tomb to be erected; and gave
to the monastery a hundred florins of rent for
ever. But if the parents live not (whom she
may corporally serve, assist, and cherish), this
counsel may fitly be applied to their souls; for
widows rarely see their parents live, being for the
most part parents themselves.

In her love and regard to the duke her son,
and likewise to his son, her grandchild, when he
was young and capable of instruction, her care
and vigilance were more than ordinary or natural;
for no occasion might make her omit her virtuous
advices and admonitions (yea, even when they
were men and married) to serve God and live
virtuously. And for example among many, this
passed in mine own hearing. When the duke
that now is, her grandson, was honoured with
the knighthood and habit of St. James, and

solemnly invested in the church of St. Dominic
in Madrid; the solemnity being done, he coming
to his grandmother the duchess (for her house
was near to it) with his red cross on his breast,
she congratulating his new honour spoke to him
in effect these words: " Son, you are now a new
man; for in taking this habit, you are entered
into many new obligations; and all are to bind
you to be a faithful and valorous knight in the
service of Almighty God and His Church. This
cross upon your breast is to put you in remembrance under Whose banner you serve, and
Whose soldier you are; and so a motive to have
Him always before your eyes Who by His death
made the Cross honourable, as you have it for an
honour to wear it where you do. And since that
His greatest enemy is sin, it is your part to fight
and war always against sin; for otherwise it will
be but false dealing to bear His colours and yield
to His enemy. Good son, reflect upon this, and
do your best to put it in practice, and you will be
honoured both of God and men. And so God
Almighty give you the joy I wish you with it."
And then she kissed his cheek. And so with
tenderness on both sides she gave and he took
her blessing upon his knee.

The Lady Hungerford, as hath been said, was her only sister by father and mother, who married with an unkind husband. She being oppressed by him for her conscience, with his permission, in 1571, came over into Flanders; where being ill-paid (or not at all paid,) that which was promised and was due to her from her husband, and too much neglected by her friends in England, found to her death the cherishing love of her sister the duchess in so favourable and continuing bounty with great affection, as she deducted from her own maintenance to assist her, as I know and have seen by many specialties performed to her, both in life and death.

Among others that attended the duchess out of England was Mrs. Margaret Harrington, sister to the Lord Harrington, her cousin german. She married her to a noble gentleman of worth, Don Benito Cisneros, and gave her in dowry twenty thousand ducats. She at her death, acknowledging the great favours and bounty she had received from the duchess, (having before buried her husband and two children she had by him,) for gratitude, with her means remaining, founded in *Zafra* the greatest part of a monastery of religious women of the holy Order of St. Francis, where her body lies buried. The duchess being in the estate of widowhood for so many years and in the many troubles that happened, such as sickness and other temporal crosses, to such as were dearest unto her; in all, ever shewed great example of Christian patience and confidence in Almighty God; and particularly in the death of the duke, her only son. Hereof I was an eye-witness. By his death she was not only left without a son, but without any living or estate in the world to maintain her. For her allowance, by her own request and assignment, was allotted her out of the Encomienda[1] of Segura, which, the duke dying, fell into the king's hands, wholly to be disposed where the king pleased. And with the heavy news of the duke's death, she not knowing his testament, nor what he might appoint for her, now seventy years of age, in a strange country, deprived of her son, wholly destitute of living, and without notice of any certain means for the sustenance of her and her family, yet fainted not in the trust of her certain Refuge, commending all to His Divine Providence, saying confidently : "Lord, Thy holy Will be done." But the duke had ordained and com-

[1] Already explained, see p. 124.

manded that she should be supplied and provided for to content, charging his son to fulfil it.

The persecution of Catholics in her country was a great affliction to her; that many times with tears and hearty compassion did she hear and report their troubles; yet her resolution was ever, saying, "Let us hope and trust in God; He will deliver us. The conversion of our country will be God Almighty's own work; therefore whosoever goes about upon their own valour, learning, devices, inventions, or any. practice whatsoever to reduce it, as stealing the honour from God to this their drift and invention, it will not succeed. Our sins made the ruin, but God must and will restore the building. In the meanwhile let us hope and trust in His Divine mercy, expecting His heavenly pleasure, not omitting to pray daily and implore His goodness, and other good men to use their labours and learning to win souls, as out of foreign seminaries they have happily begun." A worthy speech and resolution in the trust of Almighty God.

CHAPTER XII.

THE ARM OF THE DUCHESS IS BROKEN. HER
SUBSEQUENT ILLNESS. HER ORDINARY MODE
OF LIFE DURING HER WIDOWHOOD.

UPON St. Bernard's day, the 20th of August,
1609, the Duchess of Infantadzo, coming to visit
her, the Duchess of Feria received her in the
hall, they both contending to give in courtesy
each other the precedence, our duchess carrying
her left arm in a scarf by reason of a pain she
had in her breast on that side, (for that the
stirring of her arm might not offend her breast,
which also was much weakened, the pain of the
breast decaying the strength of it,) the Duchess
of Infantadzo taking her by that hand would put
her before her; which doing with some force, the
other pulling her arm back, so wrested between
both, broke the bone a little above the elbow; at
which suddenly our duchess gave a sighing groan,
saying "*Mi braço està quebrado*" (My arm is

broken). I, being the next before the duchess, astonished at the sudden cry and complaint, not imagining it could be broken with so small a violence, rather thinking it might be put out of joint, called her women, who came to her, and taking her arm affirmed the same. The pain being extreme, servants were sent with all speed to find a bone-setter, and advised to a lame one who was said to be skilful. The first found came to her, took her in hand, and said it was broken; but the unskilful fellow, lame of both his legs, handled her very roughly. She was forced to apply her body, weak and full of pain, to his hands; which he, tying up very rudely and imperfectly, to her exceeding dolour, she complaining of his unskilfulness, his rude handling and the extreme pain he put her to; the duke her grandson being then called and present, and likewise the physician, who much reproving him for the undertaking and performing it so unworthily, was made to leave her, and present commandment was given to seek the king's bone-setter, one called Cuença; who being found after much seeking, came instantly, late at night. He unbinding her arm, exclaimed against the unskilfulness of the former surgeon, felt it splintered, and so bound it up in the presence of the physicians, all visiting her together twice or thrice a day.

Yet this bone-setter's skill proved not so good; for she remained still with extremity of pain and without rest, still complaining that the bone was not well set. Which a lady, a kinswoman of the Duke, feeling, wished that a bone-setter out of the country, whom she had tried, might be sent for; commending him much both for his skill and good fortune in his cures. This man dwelt twenty-six or twenty-seven leagues from Madrid. I presently sent for him with the most speed that might be; who arrived within three days, a plain country fellow, who would not touch her but in the presence of the physicians, for which we liked him the better. He asked her Grace of the manner of her pain, and where it most afflicted her, and at the coming of the physician he unbound her arm and palpably showed the error of the cure, which the physicians plainly saw; and all present with the touch of the hand might perceive that a splint of the cracked bone stood out and was not fixed in its place. And this was seven or eight days after the first dressing; in which time may be supposed the great pain she passed, in so deli-

cate and aged a body of seventy-two years. This
man dressed it, bound it up and took upon him
the cure; the king's bone-setter being dismissed.

The good duchess remained afterwards from
this time forty days together in her bed in one
posture, without turning her; for if she stirred,
the pain of her arm would force her to lie still on
her back; notwithstanding, in these extremities,
marvellous was her hope and confidence in
Almighty God, passing all with quiet and admirable sufferance and patience, as the holy Tobias.
For whereas she had always feared God from her
infancy, and kept His commandments, she repined
not against God because of the trouble which had
befallen her, but continued immovable in the
fear of God all the days of her life.[1]   In
these pains of her arm and breast, and all
other adverse chances whatsoever, either corporal
or external, she always with a notable conformity
submitted herself to the will of our Lord, beseeching His Divine Majesty to do with her as might
be most pleasing to His holy service and to the
salvation of her soul; and daily, (but chiefly
when these pains most troubled and tormented
her) did she repeat this sentence in the Spanish

[1] See Tobias ii. 13, 14.

tongue, written with her own hand in her book of flowers. "Lord, Thou knowest what is convenient for the health of my soul; I beseech Thee so to succour my corporal necessities as I may not lose the spiritual."

The first place of visit that she made going out of her house after this painful accident, which was the 26th of October following, was a pilgrimage to the chapel of our Blessed Lady at a monastery of the Dominicans called Atocha, a place of great concourse and devotion. By which, and many other troublesome occurrences that came upon her in this her widow's estate, doth notably appear the lively trust and Christian hope she had in God Almighty, as will likewise be seen in her last sickness.

I might compare this good duchess in her way of living to the notablest matrons that have been in the Christian world. For ordinarily, if possibility of health suffered, she rose with the day in summer and in winter before day, and being soon ready, she went into her oratory, where she remained until she had heard Mass. For between seven and eight o'clock in summer-time, but in the winter somewhat later, her chaplain came to say Mass; and if both chaplains were at home they

both said Mass, and often other priests and
religious came thither, and ordinarily she heard
all.   And having heard Mass she called such
servants as had the guiding of her affairs to know
how business went, and to appoint what should
be done.   She daily read the Office of our Blessed
Lady, the Office of the Holy Cross, and of the
Holy Ghost; at certain times the whole Office of
the Dead, and the Gradual Psalms, and on some
certain special feasts the whole Office of the
Breviary.   She no day omitted to say the general
litanies, and other particular litanies as the day
and time required.   She weekly, and all the
feasts of the year, frequented the holy Sacraments of Confession and Communion.   Never
was she idle, but was either praying, working,
reading or disposing the affairs of her house,
except when strangers or persons of quality came
to visit her, or she in correspondent courtesy
went to visit them; which time she often complained was burdensome to her.   After that her
sight was not so good to work curious works, she
employed her labour to work for the poor; and
the last she did was to sew and hem sheets for
the hospital.   Her other former works were
sumptuous and precious, wrought for God's

service and the use of the Church; and the last
she worked were the ornaments for priest and
altar given by her to the new English seminary
in Madrid.

All the solemn and principal feasts of the year
she failed not to hear even-song and High Mass
in the monastery of St. Dominic, or of the
Angels, being Franciscan nuns in the same
street; where the offices were performed with
great solemnity, music, and devotion; and she
continued there, the whole office being very long.
In the Holy Week she was in a manner continually in the church; and the latter four days
spent daily there ten or eleven hours.

When her sight failed to see to work, as I say,
she passed the most time in reading devout and
spiritual books, as the *Meditations of St. Augustine,* his *Confessions,* and the *Manual,* in the
Spanish tongue; the lives of Saints, which she
daily read herself, being well; and in her weakness they were read to her in the hearing of her
women servants. She had ever with this devotion
all true humility. She was an enemy to vanity
and flattery; yet could not be hidden, as many
religious and persons of the best fame desired to
be remembered in her prayers, as did that holy

nun of St. Francis' Order in Carion de los Condes, whom for rare sanctity and true heavenly virtues, the wisest, learnedest, religiousest, and mightiest in Spain, did admire, whom the king and queen went often to visit and to be partaker of her counsel and prayers. This religious virgin did sometimes write to the duchess, desiring correspondence by letters, some whereof I have seen, and was astonished at the style, to see a woman write with so high wisdom of Divine reasons and counsels of perfection, which to me showed an apostolic spirit. Divers Popes have written particular Briefs to the duchess, commending themselves to her prayers; as Pope Gregory XIII., Pope Sixtus V., Pope Clement VIII., whose letters I have seen and read.[8]

The noble widows of Spain, by a laudable and worthy custom observed among them, are free of the fondness and blemish of affecting worldly fashions; for after the death of their husbands, they retire themselves from all worldly vanity and ostentation, their apparel being the plainest and cheapest stuffs, never wearing gold, silver, jewel, silk or lace. Their own lodgings are

---

[8] Namely, one of Pope Paul the Fifth, dated at St. Mark's, Rome, 1st May, 1607.

L

hanged in winter with plain, coarse black cloth, and in hotter weather with buckrams, or such coarse poor stuffs. Their servants and attendants had but what was necessary, without show of light bravery. Their own upper garments were worn under a coarse black mantle, a toke of white linen that covers all their person. And seldom or never do they take another husband, except they be heirs, very young and without children. I know a lady, the only daughter of the Marquis of Velada, majordomo mayor to the king, married at eighteen years of age to the Duke of Medina Celi. Before the year came about she had a son and the duke her husband died. She could not be brought to marry again, nor would give her son another father; holding it much dishonour and disparagement to their person, house and children, to marry again. For the law saith : "A woman passing to second vows neglecteth the three best things—God, the memory of her deceased husband, and the love of her children."

Our duchess, when her husband died, was in the thirty-fourth year of her age, mother of one only son, then twelve years old; the duke not above fifty when he died; which, comparing all

their ages together, seemed to be the time that
the delight and comfort of each other should
have been most. She in her husband, not yet
begun to be old; in her son, now growing to
years of understanding; the duke in her, now
married to her thirteen years; now well acquainted with the language, air, customs and
conditions of that country; and the more for
that he was then named and appointed by the
king for governor of the Low-Countries, where
they should have lived so near to England and to
her friends. Herein they both took (as the
duchess told me) an extraordinary consolation;
for the duke, being then with the king, wrote
the Parabien [4] of the news to her, willing her to
advertise her grandmother, who then was alive
at Louvain. But the duchess, although most
glad with the news, wrote again to the duke: "I
dare not write it to my grandmother, lest something might succeed to cross it; and she, crossed
in the joyful expectation, might turn to the
prejudice of her health and life. And being the
most comfortable news to my temporal desires
which I have heard since my coming out of

---

[4] Parabien is explained by the dictionary of the Spanish
Academy as meaning Congratulation, Felicitation.

England, yet I dare not believe it, until we be
in the way; lest believing it and not succeeding,
I should do myself no little harm." And these
crosses succeeded that her grandmother died the
same month of July, and the duke in September
following. The son also seemed to be in forward
happiness, being in the age to know the worth of
his father and the goodness and virtue of his
mother. But these delights and comforts were
all wholly dashed with the state of a widow,
who never after took delight in the world but for
the breeding of her son, as was fitting his years
and quality; in all things banishing from herself,
both in clothing and diet, all that might show
deliciousness.

In the year 1588, when that famous hypocrisy
of the Dominican nun of Lisbon, who pretended
the ambition of a Saint, called Soror Maria de
Visitaçion, was discovered; who by pricking her
head with thorns, by wounding her side and hands
to the imitation of St. Francis and St. Catharine
of Sienna, by putting herself to grievous smart for
this ambitious vanity, would persuade the world
that they were by some sovereign apparition so
fixed in her body as they were in those glorious
Saints, and by counterfeit raptures, had procured

such an esteem as from all parts of Spain they
sent and came to her to have her benediction
and some linen clothes sprinkled with the blood
of her wounds ; which she carried so cunnningly,
as all in a manner held her for a Saint. The
king himself, Philip II., albeit very incredulous in
such matters, but upon firm evidences and testimonies admitted by the Church, yet by sundry
relations made to his majesty began to give credit
to this so general report of the nun. And I have
heard by some, (whether true or no, I know not),
that in the year 1588, when that great Spanish
fleet went for England, many of the banners
were carried to her to bless (a great rashness
and presumption in her to do it), being, as she was,
a mere hyprocrite, shortly after found out and
proved : and after strict examination, being Prior-
ess then of the monastery, confessed by herself
(the same year, the 15th of October) that these
were devices of her invention to be accounted a
Saint. The story is notorious, and had deceived
many wise, great, learned and good Religious.
She, being convicted, was chastised and was very
penitent, refusing no penance, but desiring as
much as flesh and blood might bear.

But to our purpose. While the fame thus ran

of her wounds and of her sanctity, and was generally so reputed, a great Religious man who had seen her and such effects as induced the credit of her supposed sanctity, being with the duchess, she asked some particulars about her, and among the rest of her conversation and diet, whether he knew anything of her in the one and observed her in the other, he being of the same Order. He answered: " Madam, your question is worth the moving, which made me at first to doubt her before I saw the effects, because she converses with most that seek her, especially such as are of reckoning, and spends much time in conversation. For her diet; she being the Superior in the Convent and held so holy, I know she hath many dainties sent her, and I hear not that she depriveth herself of any part of that which the monastery and the Order allows her." Our Duchess replied. " Is it so? I fear this sanctity is temporal, and will not long last. For all Saints, memorable to have been great servants of God Almighty, have had their eminence in these two virtues. For their private persons, recollection and abstinence, properly united to the true service of His Divine Majesty, but when necessity and charity enforced. And the contrary (to wit, conversation and dainties, with variety of gustful diet) were baits to worldly love and inducements to sin ; " alleging the example of St. Martin and the holy woman that excused herself to see him ; of St. Francis, St. Dominic, St. Clare and others.

The love of chastity and of chaste persons in the duchess I have noted before. The least gesture of the contrary either in shew or speech was marvellously displeasing to her; she commending very often the pure and clean soul of Queen Mary her mistress, whose education had been so chaste and innocent of impurity as she knew not the meaning of sluttish terms or foul, unchaste words, as I touched in the description of her life.

I will add here what an ancient lady in England did tell me of her before my coming to Spain, who was a courtier. Queen Mary being in the gallery ready to go to the chapel, within the traverse, the Lord William Howard,[5] Lord Chamberlain being with her, he taking his leave ; without the traverse stood the maids of honour,

[5] Lord William Howard's name occurs very frequently in the Privy Purse Expenses of the Princess Mary, and in such terms as to show that he was a frequent visitor in her household.

expecting to wait on the queen to the chapel. Mrs. Frances Neville[6] standing next to the traverse, the Lord Chamberlain passing by, a merry gentleman, took her by the chin, saying: "My pretty . . . .[7] how dost thou?" Which the queen saw and heard, the traverse being drawn. The queen gone forth, finding her farthingale at her foot loose, made sign to Mrs. Neville to pin it, which, kneeling down, she did. The queen then took her by the chin, as he had done saying, "God-a-mercy, my pretty. . . ." She hearing the queen say thus, so blushed as she seemed to be astonished, replying: "Madam, what says your majesty?" still upon her knees, and seemed to be much troubled. The queen answered, "What is the matter? Have I said or done more than the Lord Chamberlain did? And may not I be as bold with thee as he?" She replied: "My Lord Chamberlain is an idle gentleman, and we respect not what he saith or doth; but your majesty, from whom I think never any heard such a word, doth amaze me either in jest or earnest to be called so by you." A . . . is a

[6] Possibly the lady who is mentioned in the same Privy Purse Expenses, pp. 192, 196, 197, 198.

[7] The expression here used will not bear repetition.

wicked misliving woman. The queen took it,
"Thou must forgive me; for I meant thee no
harm."

Thus chaste were the thoughts and words
of this renowned princess and such was the
reputation of her family, in which chaste school
was bred this our duchess; excellently well
learning her lesson and imitating her mistress as in her will and purpose she did exceedingly abhor and detest all impurities and
unclean words. And I have known that she
hath plainly, yet with reserved modesty, told
great men of note and worth the dishonour and
misery they purchased to themselves by the base
actions of unchaste lives; and would boldly
reprove such with whom she had any interest of
friendship. Nor were any, of what degree soever,
who had the fame of such a life, ever welcome to
her. And being by chance told that certain
women were met in the duke her grandson's
coach, that had not the best reputation, she
would never afterwards enter again into that
coach. Divers of our noble English gentlemen,
at their being in the court of Spain and visiting
her, admired in her this virtue, so carried with
such a graceful manner as they wished that she

might for a time live in her own country to be
an example of imitation to our great ladies. It
is the virtue that setteth out and adorneth all
other virtues, especially in women, being the
speech of the body and the interpreter of the
mind.

A lie was most odious to her, which in her
pages and younger sort she would have sharply
chastised as an enormous fault. And the servant
that she found to have told her an untruth fell
much from her favour, she holding it a vice most
unworthy of a Christian. She, faithful and
punctual in promises, advised before what she
promised, held it a chief point of honour and
religion to perform it. And for facility in giving
credit to the reports of others, she measured them
by her own intentions, observing this columbine
and candidous simplicity under the rule of charitable construction; albeit in matters that imported the honour of God, the government of her
weightier affairs, her credulity was not so great
and facile, but directed by the rule of God's
Church and discussed with that prudence as she
would not easily be deceived or over-reached.

Of mildness had she great use at her first
coming into Spain, particularly among the kin-

dred of the duke her husband, his mother then
living; who was not pleased with the match, for
that she had purposed to marry the duke with
her grandchild, the daughter of Count Don Pedro,
her eldest son. But the duke, avoiding and pre-
venting so near a match in blood as his niece,
married as he did; which so angered his mother
as she married her to his younger brother (as
hath been said) and passed to him the Marquis-
ship of Pliego, an estate of one hundred thousand ducats by the year, and so made
a suit between the two brothers. Yet the
duchess carried herself towards her mother-
in-law, with that mildness and affable respect
as it afterwards grieved the Marquesa of
what she had done; and she continued to
the children of the younger brother (whereof
I am a witness) that love and regard as if her
husband had suffered no wrong by their father,
and the like to all the kindred; notwithstanding
the suit was on foot between her son and his
cousin-german, the heir of that house; so gracious
and mild was she in forgetting injuries.

CHAPTER XIII.

ANECDOTES OF HER MANAGEMENT OF CHILDREN.
OF THE RELEASE OF ENGLISH PRIŞONERS. OF
THE QUEEN OF SCOTLAND. HER LIBERALITY
TO THE POOR AND TO CHURCHES AND HOS-
PITALS.

I HAVE before showed the bringing up of her son
and the pious government of her house, family
and children; yet I may not omit a discreet
policy that she used in the education of the
dukes, her son and grandson, to make them follow
their book and apply their lessons.

Their first exercise in the morning was to hear
Mass, which was done before eight o'clock. Then
they went to their book, their master being in the
house, he read them their lesson; which heard
and they able to construe, they broke their fast.
Then were they set a task, which they were to
repeat to their master before dinner. When dinner was ready and to be brought in, she asked
their master if they had done their lessons. If

yea, all well; and there was some reward, or contentment, commending their diligence; if no, the
duchess commanded presently not to bring in the
meat, telling them with a sweet reprehension,
" Although you will not dine yourselves; yet keep
not me from my dinner at a due time; for I must
not nor can eat until you have done your lessons
and said your book as you ought; and so I, your
mother, (when he learned, to her son; and to her
grandson, I your grandmother) an old woman,
must be punished for your negligence. You see my
care is that you want nothing that is fit for you,
and I must want my meat for your play and idleness. Go to your study and make an end quickly
that the meat be not spoiled, for we must all fast
till you have done." Which served as a prudent
correction and discreet encouragement to them to
apply to their books, and diligently to perform
their studies in due time.

I showed before the singular zeal this lady and
the duke her husband used in the time of Lent,
and especially in the Holy Week, and the great
feasts of the year, with marvellous devotion, humility and charity to the poor Descalços Friars.
De La Lapa, in serving them and feeding them.
And it is very ordinary among the great ladies in

Spain to visit hospitals and to give the sick and diseased to eat with their own hand, to serve them, to wipe their sores, to cleanse their wounds, to feed and cherish them with such alacrity and humble diligence as evidently sheweth that it proceedeth from true fervour of Christian devotion and piety, which is really to wash the feet of saints.

The Cardinal of Rhemes calleth our duchess another Queen Helena, who with liberal bounty employed her goods to succour the Scots, English and Irish, and other afflicted and fugitive Catholics, who had recourse into Spain for the exercise of their faith and religion. At one time she procured the release of thirty-eight Englishmen, prisoners in Seville, being all taken in the West Indies and sentenced to die, and some merchants accused for assisting them with shipping and other provision for that voyage. As one Mr. Norris, a merchant of Barnstaple in Devonshire, and sometime Mayor of that town, and one of that company, hath told me, much magnifying the charity and affection of the duchess to her distressed countrymen, and the obligation that he and his followers had to her for their lives and liberty. At divers other times,

especially after the differences grew to professed
quarrels between the crowns of England and
Spain, sundry such adverse accidents falling out,
men having recourse to our duchess, by her
mediation had their release procured and their
present extremities assisted with liberal benevolence, although I hold few of these for saints; yet
because they fell into trouble, she of her goodness
was forward to help them; which I think Sir
Richard Hawkins of Plymouth, prisoner in
Madrid in the latter time of Queen Elizabeth,
will acknowledge.

But to come to a saint, (one who at least died
a saint and martyr) when the Queen of Scots,
forced by her rebellious subjects to leave her
country, had fled into England, expecting there
to have refuge and assistance, according to
promise, found the contrary, to wit, restraint
and such other hard measure as her rents out of
France came not to her; which our good duchess
understanding, solicited the duke her husband,
then living, in her behalf, who sent her twenty
thousand ducats to relieve her present necessities.

If acts of charity to Catholic priests and gentlemen of our country, whom domestic calamities
and oppressions caused to seek refuge abroad,

should be here particularly set down, I should enter into a large narration, and could myself declare many particulars, the bounty of which pious actions has passed to many by my hands. But in so doing I should do wrong to the godly intention of the good lady, although deceased, who could not endure to have such deeds numbered nor yet remembered, who not willingly would have their own names, or the names of their friends, mentioned in this kind. This our good duchess had spared much from the lustre of herself, both for diet (in which she was marvellous temperate) and for other appurtenances to her person, to be able to do the more good works.

It hath fallen out in the time that I served her often, and was her usual custom, when any gentleman of quality that she knew and had any acquaintance with her, that lay sick and was thought to be in want, she commanded her steward, or the gentleman that had the charge of the private expenses of her house, to put up (tied in a paper) a hundred crowns, or sixty, or or fifty, or forty, or thirty, or twenty, or so much as it pleased her, according to the want and condition of the party, which she would take so bound up, and put in her pocket when she went to visit the party; and after salutation and pious advices as occasion was offered, at her coming away, taking leave with words of comfort, would put the paper under the pillow of the sick person. And to others with whom she was not so well acquainted in their distress, if any spake to our duchess for them, she seldom or never denied, but they tasted her bounty according to their quality and her means. She was very respective and compassionate to such as were of noble blood and ingenuous education, who by some disaster had fallen into wants; pitying their estate that had been fed and bred with plenty and were afterward necessitated to have relief and sustenance by the alms and bounty of strangers. Of this sort, of our country, of Irish and of Spaniards and French also, I could relate them that in a high kind were beholding to the bounty of our duchess.

Her ordinary allowance was to give bread and money to the poor religious monasteries and hospitals of Madrid, and to those of St. Francis bread and eggs. An ordinary allowance of alms every month was to be given in money by the gentlewoman that kept the expenses of the house to such poor as asked at the door. Never any

M

English priest or other stranger, poor Englishman
or other that pretended need, who asked of her,
or otherwise by some of her servants desired
relief of their wants, but had from her a charitable benevolence. And seldom did she refuse
to see any Englishman who asked it, were he
never so mean. The general hospital of Madrid,
weekly, as is said, received her alms, and in
other necessities were succoured with sheets and
blankets required. Many poor widows and
orphans in the duke's estate had perpetual
maintenance by her charity. Many Sundays and
Holy-days did she send the whole supper of the
Recollects Descalços of St. Francis's Order in
Madrid with some extraordinary good supply,
being particularly devoted to that Order. For
she herself had taken the habit of the Third
Order of St. Francis and was professed in it,
wearing under her outward garment the habit
and scapulary while she lived. In suits or
pretences that any of our countrymen had in the
court of Spain, very forward was she, if they
sought it, with her best means to assist them, to
write in their favour to the Lords of the Council,
and to send some friend or servant with them to
further their business. And such as wanted

found other aidful relief. Thus was she daily in doing good works.

If her means had answered her desires for the founding, furnishing and adorning of monasteries, she had been one of the notablest patronesses in the Christian world, wholly addicted to the service of God and the glorifying of His eternal Name. I have heard our duchess say that if in her time, our kingdom should be so happy as to admit the public face of Catholic Religion again, she would endeavour to be the first with the poor means she had to build a monastery of St. Francis's Order and completely to furnish it; knowing and acknowledging the general good that those Religious do in a christian country; and while she lived she built the monastery of Monte-Virgine of that Order, Descalços Recollects, and Santa Marina in *Zafra*, Nuns of the Order of St. Clare. Through the whole course of her life she was not sparing in advancing these good works; as in repairing St. Onophrio de la Lapa, our Lady del Rosario of St. Dominic; in furnishing these and others with rich ornaments, costly pictures; devout confraternities; as all the churches and monasteries in *Zafra* and all in the duke's estate have her in perpetual memory.

Also she procuring from the Apostolic See great
privileges and indulgences for their better estab-
lishing, continuance and increase; the effect
whereof the great church of *Zafra* and Sta. Clara,
an ancient rich monastery of Franciscan Nuns
in that town, do largely enjoy.   Fray Juan Baptista Moles saith (in his book and chapter before
alleged), "There are two hermitages, one very
ancient and dedicated to St. Onophrio and St.
Paul the first hermit; and the other, which the
duchess, the Lady Jane Dormer, built to St. John
the Evangelist, very beautiful, pleasant and devout, which Don Juan de Ribera, Bishop of Bad-
ajos, and afterwards Archbishop of Valencia and
Patriarch of Antioch, did consecrate."   And our
duchess, in the end of her life, all that she could
leave besides her household stuff which descended to the duke, and some few remembrances left
to friends and servants (for there was no servant
that served her, at the time of her death, but
had some remembrance or legacy given him) and
besides what was bequeathed to the poor and to
say Masses for her soul, all was left to monasteries.   Yea, the annuities that she left for life to
her most obliged servants were in reversion to
the cloister of Santa Marina, in which she had

built a marvellous fair church with a fair gallery
from the duke's palace; and above, at the end of
the gallery, an oratory, from which they may hear
and see Mass at the high altar, in which work is
showed magnificence and devotion.

CHAPTER XIV.

OF THE SICKNESS AND LAST DAYS OF THE DUCHESS OF FERIA.

AFTER the breaking of her arm, the extreme pain
of her breast still continuing, our duchess daily
grew weaker, and many times with such accidents
of hot agues as in that great age and feebleness
of body she was ordered by the physicians to be
let blood. So finding herself with a perpetual
decay of strength and health she only expected
that which escapes none; having in her memory
and often repeating that of the wise man, "*Me-
morare novissima tua, et in æternum non peccabis.*"
To this end she had fastened to her beads a
death's-head (which beads she put into my hand,
dying; which I have and much esteem), on which

she meditated and often discoursed, having learnt
of St. Hierome that notable sentence: "He
easily contemns all things, whose thoughts always
tell him that he must die." And also for this
end, she had made her testament and disposed
her estate, having (as is shewed before) taken the
habit of penance of the Third Order of St. Francis,
to be participant of the graces and indulgences of
that holy religion. She had entered herself into
the list and number *de Ancillis,* or handmaids of
our Blessed Lady, when in Sta. Ursula at Alcala,
a convent of Franciscan nuns, was founded a
sisterhood or congregation of them with this title,
"to the Queen of Angels;" rejoicing to be the
Ancilla of her, by whose mediation and gracious
intercession she might attain grace to die well.
Likewise did she ordain, many months before her
death, her coffin to be made, in which her body
should be entered, which when ordered, and the
measure to be taken of her body, her women
grew tender and wept, the duchess said: "Why
weep you? For this must be, and it cannot be
long before it come—Weep not, but pray for me.
We must all die; but that which imports, is to
die well and to have a good end. And this is
that which I request of you all to commend me

to God, that He vouchsafe to give me His grace to end well."

Our duchess kept her bed almost twelve months before her death, pained through her whole body, especially in her arm that had been broken; for although it had been set and cured, yet the pain of her breast kept it very weak. And once, taking her little grand-daughter in her arms, being then the only child of the duke her grand-son, when the nurse took it from her, it so chanced as her arm a little strained, put her to that extremity of pain as she was falling down in a swoon; and after that it put her to such trouble and affliction as she could not lift it to her head, nor pluck out a pin with that hand, but carried it always in a scarf. Notwithstanding this infirmity and other exceeding dolours of her body, the same still was the exercise of her Christian virtues and her zeal to God's service; for weekly she both confessed and communicated, had daily good men with her; no day did she leave to hear Mass. For when her weakness began to be such as she could hardly remain out of her bed, by license of the vicar of the Arch-bishop of Toledo, (who himself came to see the place for the decency of it,) her oratory was removed to another part, as from her bed, through the passage that entered into her chamber, she might see the altar, hear Mass, behold and adore the holy Sacrifice, which was her true comfort; and so enjoyed it to the time of her decease, for the day that she died she heard Mass. Before her oratory was thus changed, in the summer-time she lay in a bedstead that turned with wheels, which at the time of Mass was set before the door of the oratory. But when winter came she was forced to remove to a warmer chamber; and had her oratory altered, as is said before.

In the same time of this her sickness that Father Ribadeneira, (a very reverend, wise, learned and ancient Father of the Society; for he had lived seventy-one years in the Order, much respected and reverenced by the duchess, who likewise answered her grace with the same good-will and regardful affection,) whom I mentioned before, having known her in England; she, in all important occasions advised with him, asked his counsel, he esteeming her a very true and able friend, and often visiting her as to whose favours, both in his own particular and for the benefit of his Order, he stood much beholding.

He dedicated to her (as before is noted [1]) his book
De los santos Estravagantes; to wit, such as were
not in the Roman calendars of breviaries and
missals. It fell out, I say, that this good Father,
in September, 1610, fell mortally sick; she then
also lying in her bed sick. This, among other
afflictions, she accounted not the least, to want
the assistance of so dear and esteemed a Father;
and sent often to visit him, myself being for the
most part the messenger. And the last message
he sent her was this: "Commend me much to
the duchess, and tell her that shortly we shall
see each other in Paradise." This message she
would have me repeat to her more than once,
and took in it extraordinary consolation. This
holy Father departed this world (I was present
when he died) the 22nd of September, in the
eighty-fifth year of his age, after great labours
and travels taken in his religion, many worthy
works set out by him to the edification of the
Christian world, as appeareth in the catalogue of
the writers of the Society, printed at Antwerp.[2]

[1] See p. 7.

[2] See *Catalogus Scriptorum religionis Societatis Jesu, auctore P.
Petro Ribadeneira,* p. 225—229, ed. Antv. 1613, 8vo. It is stated
in his epitaph that he died at Madrid, 22nd September, 1611.
Also *Histoire du Père Ribadeneyra,* par le Père J. M. Prat. Paris,
1862.

It pleased Almighty God, at that time also, to take out of this world the most virtuous and good Queen of Spain, who died at St. Laurence by the Escurial, the 3rd of October, 1611.[8] Which when our duchess heard, condoling the great loss of the whole kingdom; (for her majesty was not twenty-eight years complete), having so many princely children deprived of so good a mother in the flower of her age; commanding presently mourning to be made for her servants, saying: "All Spain and Germany had true cause to mourn; but she was worthy of a better kingdom, which this good lady had attained in so young years; and I, poor woman and decrepit, do languish in this bed with pain and misery." Our duchess sent me to give the *Pesumè* to the queen's ghostly Father, a Jesuit, that came with her out of Germany, condoling his and the general loss. In doing the message, he could not for tears answer me, but wept like a child.

In this extreme sickness, the pains being extraordinary that our good duchess suffered, yet when any came to visit her, were he religious, or a neighbour, or any gentlemam of our country, she received him with that alacrity and cheerfulness

[8] This was Margaret of Austria, wife of Philip III., King of Spain, and daughter of Charles, Archduke of Gratz.

of countenance, as increased an affectionate
respect from them to her. Yea, such was the
sweetness of her condition as drew a certain
reverence and esteem from them who conversed
with her; and in this conversation, such was her
mildness, gravity, and gracious deportment, as
after such visit they affected and honoured her
much more, as well might be applied to her what
the Holy Scripture saith of the noble and
memorable widow Judith: "And she was among
all most famous, because she feared our Lord
very much; neither was there that spake an ill
word of her." [4] In this sickness, marvellous was
the care our duchess took and the strict account
to make full satisfaction where any thing might
be due, not alone for matters past but for to
come, and so she had provided for the burial;
and the exact accomplishment of her testament,
having committed the charge to her faithful
servants. For the better clearing of all questions,
she wrote, some months before she died, to the
Contador and Treasurer, officers of the duke's
estate, (whereof she had been governess many
years, as hath been said) charging them before
God, that if they knew or could understand any

[4] See Judith, viii. 8.

thing wherein she might be indebted by way of justice or conscience that they should advise her; commanding them to take pains and use diligence to search and inquire if there should be any cause for restitution, and to demand and hear the complaints of all, and to advertise her that they might be remedied. These letters I wrote. And likewise did she call a servant, whom she much trusted, under whose charge passed, some years before she died, the general and great receipts and expenses of all accounts in her house, to have great care of this particular for satisfaction, commanding him to look well about and remember her where she might have any obligation. So Christian and fervent was her desire completely to satisfy with all that might be due in justice or conscience. And to her great cost did she deal with some, more by the way of pitiful than of obliged. As but three days before she died, taking compassion upon the master carpenter that had taken, too great, all the timber-work of the church of Sta. Marina, complaining that he had overshot himself in the bargain and was too great a loser, desired by way of petition to be considered. She did, having examined the business, in compassionate favour grant his suit and signed the Libranças for the recovery of this money; which the man took so gratefully when I gave him the Libranças (or warrants), wishing him to give some alms to the poor monastery in gratuity, he promised at the receipt of the money to give them a hundred ducats. Until three days before our duchess died she omitted not the saying of her usual prayers, as the Office of our Blessed Lady, her beads, and to have read to her the life of the Saint of the day. When she had not possibility of health to read her Office herself, she willed some other to read it for her.

On Thursday night, the 19th of January, her infirmity increasing, I was present while her excellency supped, which she seemed to eat with appetite and reasonable gust, her supper being a partridge and some jelly. After grace was said, she remaining sitting up in her bed, to wash her mouth and hands, as she usually did, she shewed so strangely fair with colour in her face, so clear and lively, as those who were present stood and admired at her sudden beauty; so as one said to another, " Did you ever see a fairer face? What may be the cause of this alteration? Is her grace turned young again?" And an ancient

gentlewoman in the company (I was present) was
bold to say to her, "Madam, your grace looks
strangely fair on the sudden." She only smiled
but replied nothing. One [5] of her servants that
understood somewhat of the nature of the pulse,
and in the absence of the physicians her grace
did usually command him to take hers, a little
before she went to take rest that night, taking it,
told her women at his going out of the chamber,
that my lady was not well, her pulse showed a
greater weakness; and that he perceived a certain
malicious increase of her ague. And therefore
on Friday morning very early he came to see how
she had passed that night, and what had succeeded. Then he found her pulse much worse
and her forces strangely weakened. Her grace
asked him how he liked her pulse? He answered
with leisure, not so well as he wished. She
importuned him to know the whole particular,
and charged him to tell her plainly and truly his
opinion. He told her the truth, and what he
thought. And she acknowledged that in the
same manner, or rather worse, she herself felt
that her spirits were much debilitated, and

[5] In the margin of the original MS. this is said to have been
"the author" himself.

it was pain to her to speak. When, not long
after, the physicians came to visit her, they confessed they found her much altered since the
day before ; yet gave her comfort that there was
not so great danger as she imagined. As her
weakness they said was more, so they appointed
her to drink goat's milk, fresh drawn. But perceiving these to be but delays and dilatory
medicines of doctors, feeling herself in danger,
although she yielded to what they prescribed,
having a thirsty desire to be with God, she commanded and ceased not to call upon us, until
order was given to bring her from the parish
church the Blessed Sacrament, *pro Viatico,*
albeit she had communicated but three or four
days before. This the physicians, under pretence
not to disanimate her, would have deferred,
alleging the present necessity not to be so great ;
until by more importunity of her grace, It was
brought to her on Saturday night, at nine o'clock,
which she received with marvellous gust and
devotion, answering with good memory and
zealous promptitude to all questions that are
demanded when in such case the Blessed Sacrament is administered.

In this occasion, the duke, her grandson, came

to ask her blessing upon his knees, and forgiveness of all displeasures and offences, offering himself, his service, and his goods, to accomplish all that her excellency should order and command; and with this grew tender. She took this offer with an affectionate impression, although she intended to charge him with nothing, only commended to him her servants and gave him her blessing with much goodwill and love of a mother, adding some short lessons of good counsel.

That night she passed resting very little, spending most of the time in prayer and hearkening to the Religious men that were about her; for almost continually from this evening to her decease there were with her two Fathers of the Society, four Franciscan friars, one Dominican Father, her chaplain, and myself.

On Sunday, the extremity increasing, she desired with great instance the Sacrament of Extreme Unction, which was brought and given her at ten o'clock in the forenoon; which likewise she received with great devotion and demonstration of her Christianity. And with others that were present when they gave her this Sacrament, was Don Juan Idiaques, an ancient councillor of

Estate, President of the Council of Orders and generally of great name and respect in Spain, who after that she had received the Sacrament, went to her bedside to kiss her hands and to take his last leave. To him standing upon his knees, (for he would not be entreated to stand otherwise) she made a speech; with so good words and reasons commending to his favour and protection, her house and the duke her grandson, as the President remained as it were amazed to see so great weakness and together such an understanding and memory in her affairs. He shedding many tears on going out of her chamber, said to us, "It is a thing to praise God for, to see this lady how well she stands with God, and the spirit that she hath."

After her grace had received this Sacrament, her servants came to her chamber to ask forgiveness and to take her blessing. There was nothing seen nor heard but tears and sighs. To all did she give pardon with gracious countenance and very good will, willing them all to pray for her. Likewise most of the great ladies that were in Madrid came to take their last leave and ask her blessing. Such was the reverence of her age, the example of her life and regard of her virtue.

N

The same afternoon an English knight, a
kinsman of our duchess, Sir Robert Chamberlain,[6]
came also to take his leave; a chief motive of his
coming to Madrid, as he said, was to kiss her
hand. He now sorry to see her in that plight,
so near her end, beseeched her blessing, and to
command him something in her service. She
said to him: "Cousin, you see my speech begins
to fail me; but what I wish you is, that you look
to it, to stand strong and firm in the Catholic
Faith. I know well that Catholics suffer great
troubles in England; but take care you lose not
the goods of heaven for the goods of the earth.
And so God Almighty bless you and keep you;"
commanding after a jewel to be given him of
one hundred ducats, which, after her death, I
bought and gave him.

That night between eight and nine o'clock she
had a trance, so extreme and violent that we all
thought it would have ended her. And while she
was in the combat of this fit, not altogether losing
her sense, the Religious about her called to her to

6 A letter from Sir John Digby to the Earl of Salisbury,
from Madrid, dated 19th January, 1612, st. vet. mentions the
arrival there of Sir Robert Chamberlain, and the death of the
chess on the night of Monday, 13th January.

name Jesus; if she could not with her tongue,
yet with her mind to call upon Him and to trust
in His Sacred Passion, putting in her hand a
little crucifix which she often kissed, embraced
it; and when she recovered her speech repeated
verbatim the words that the Fathers had said to
her, and of herself (only with perfect memory) the
whole hymn, *O Gloriosa Domina, Excelsa super
sidera*, etc.; and many times repeated

> Maria, Mater gratiæ,
> Mater misericordiæ;
> Tu nos ab hoste protege,
> Et hora mortis suscipe.
> Crux Christi, protege nos;
> Crux Christi, salva nos;
> Crux Christi, defende nos.

And in a manner her speech was always: " Jesu,
Maria, be with me; Mother of God, help me;
good Jesu, deliver me from these troubles." And
in this sort, taking at times a little broth of
substance passed to the next morning; excusing
herself to the Religious that had taken such pains
with her that night. And in this interim, that
night she spake promptly and readily of divers
things with the servant[7] whom she trusted, com-

[7] Most probably the author himself.

mending to his charge certain alms of much charity to divers persons.

This day, Monday, being the last day of her life in this world, and in Spain a holiday of St. Hildefonsus, Bishop of Toledo, which at midnight she had mind of; for such was then her memory, as knowing it to be passed twelve o'clock, she said to me: " This is now St. Hildefonsus's day; to-morrow, Tuesday, our Blessed Lady of Peace (for so it is observed in the archbishopric of Toledo); Wednesday, St. Paul's day; and Thursday, the 26th of January, St. Polycarpus's day, the day that my son died in Naples." This day, I say, being holiday, she called and took care all her people should hear Mass. And when she saw the priest vested, she asked me, if all her women were there? Which Mass, notwithstanding being so weak and lying in her bed, she attended and heard with great devotion. About twelve o'clock the same day, a paroxysm or trance came upon her, so violent as she seemed to be wholly without sense and breathing to the last of her life; so as we all held her for departed; until, after a little space, they named, with a loud voice, the Name of Jesus, she a little bowed down her head without any other motion, and continued in this trance very near an hour.

When she was come to herself and had taken a little broth, the young duchess, her daughter-in-law, told her that the Lady Digby, wife of the English Lord Ambassador, had been there to see her grace, but finding her in that agony was returned home. Her grace answered, " I would I had seen her." The duchess presently with haste sent her coach for her, sending her word that her grace was yet alive, and if she would come, might see her. The lady came as soon as she heard it, with all possible expedition. And coming into our duchess' chamber, drew near to the bedside, other company that were there giving her place. It seemed by her grace's countenance that she was glad of her coming; and after salutations, the one bidding welcome, the other condoling to see her so sick, our duchess said to her these words: "Lady, I speak with much difficulty; and that which I have not strength to say I refer to this Father; " for there stood at her bed's head, Father Creswell, an English Father of the Society.[8] "Your Lady-

---

[8] Father Joseph Creswell, S.J. See De Backer, 1—1464, Oliver, 1—78.

ship is now come into a country and place of
Catholics where you may see and learn ; and if you
do not, the fault is yours.   And believe me, Lady,
and I do tell it you, dying, *That there is no salvation
out of the Catholic Roman Church* ; nor true faith
but that which Catholics profess.   And if your
ladyship desires to save your · soul, look to this
which imports you."   The Lady Digby answered :
" Madame, I desire nothing so much, as reason
is I should, as the salvation of my soul ; and I
trust that the Lord will have mercy upon me ;
for in the law and religion wherein I have been
bred, I desire to serve Him."   Her grace replied :
" Lady, desires are not enough, it is necessary to
put it into work, and no work is good but that
which is by the faith and teaching of the Church.
I lack strength to speak more ; look well to it ;
this is it which most imports you."   And so bade
her farewell ;   the Lady Ambassador weeping
very much to see our Duchess draw so near to
her end.

When the Lady Digby was gone, one that stood
on the further side of the bed, which was towards the wall, asked her Grace[9] how she did,

---

[9] Here again we recognise the writer of this narrative, and
in the incident recorded a few lines afterwards.

and where she had been an hour since (meaning
when she was in that great trance), telling her
that we all thought she had been in heaven.
She answered: " Surely, I was very near, why
did they call me back again?" Which was no
small comfort to me and all that heard it. An
hour after, she turned again into another trance,
but not so violent as was the last; for she had her
sense and always showed signs of devotion when
they named Jesus or Maria, with bowing down
her head and opening her eyes towards heaven.
After a little time, her speech returning again,
the same party came to her Grace, offering his
service in what she pleased to command, and
withal asked what she would have? She answered in English. "Health (pausing a little,
added) in heaven, which I hope will quickly
come; for we are in the Vespers of our Lady of
Peace,[10] who in peace will receive my soul this
night. Jesus, Maria, be with me. Sweet Jesus,
have mercy on me."

A little time after, they brought to her the two
young grandchildren, the daughters of the duke,

[10] A marginal note here tells us that on "the twenty-fourth
of January, in the diocese of Toledo, is celebrated the feast of
our Lady of Peace."

her grandson. She gave them her blessing, asking it from heaven for them and for herself, which was not far off; for then, her spirits beginning to fail, within a matter of two hours after (that time being spent by the Religious about her in godly exhortations, prayers, and Divine service used in such occasions), a little after nine o clock in the night on the 23rd of January, 1612, sweetly without any trouble more than the pangs of death, which were very short, she rendered her blessed soul to God for to live with Him eternally.

CHAPTER XV.

ACCOUNT OF THE FUNERAL OF THE DUCHESS, AND THE CIRCUMSTANCES CONNECTED WITH IT.

THUS, our virtuous duchess left this transitory world to receive the reward of her virtue with the Saints of God, whereof we may have more than probable or moral hope that she was soon made partaker, considering what passed in the foresaid trances. She had suffered many months of purgatory in this world; led a laudable and exemplary christian life; and ended it with much edification and consolation of all the assistants; for when her tongue failed, which was some half-hour before she deceased, her hands and eyes showed her faith and desire to be with God. And the last temporal thing that she spoke when her speech began to fail her was to her maid who attended at her bed's feet, bidding her to put in decency and handsomely her bed-clothes about

her body, to the end, no doubt, she might die with
seemly decency so as to prevent what perhaps
the pangs of death might cause.

So this our duchess, on the octave of her birth
(for she was born on the sixth of February), did
return her happy soul to her Creator to attain the
sum of her felicity; and left her body remaining,
with the face so beautiful, her hands so fair and
flexible, wonderful in that great age, that they
seemed rather of a heavenly creature than of a
dead body. So dressed up in a poor Franciscan
habit, which she had kept by her many years for
that purpose to be her outward shroud (which
had been the cast garment of a holy good Friar)
and with a scapular of St. Dominic's Order, she
was laid thus upon a pallet with her face un-
covered and her hands held up close together, as
the use is to hold them praying.

In the meantime the duke, her grandson, being
there, the Teniente of the town was called, (who
is the judge in civil causes) and the scrivener
that had written and sealed up her testament, to
unseal it, open it, and read it publicly before the
said Teniente, the duke, and others appointed.
For so had our duchess ordained, that as soon as
she should be departed this world, the duke (if

he were in the town) should be present at the
reading of her testament to ratify it if he pleased
or otherwise, if he should take any exceptions
about any legacies, to shew the cause before the
Justice. When the Teniente was come before
the duke, the Marquis de Malpica, the Conde de
los Arcos, Don Alonso de Cordova, Don Francisco
Garnica and others, where I was also present,
the testament was opened and read aloud by the
scrivener ; which all heard with attention, the
reading of it continuing about an hour. Which
when read, the Teniente asked the duke if his
excellency would ratify and confirm it ? He
answered, " Most willingly," and then subsigned
it with his hand. The Teniente, also signing it,
said, " I see no other defect in this testament but
one, that it is not printed, that others might learn
by it to make their testament ; because I see in
it the lively points and effects of great charity,
rare wisdom, worthy virtue and true Christian
zeal." This said the judge of the town of Madrid.
The conclusion of which testament I will add
here, being directed to the duke her grandson,
her heir, as her last blessing, translated out of
the Spanish, which is as follows, *verbatim* :—

"After having commended my soul to our

Lord, for the love and most intimate affection I
bear to the duke, Don Gomez, as my grandchild,
and lord of the house of his father, I require and
beseech and charge him, that he take for foundation of all his actions the holy fear of our Lord
God; having care to give no place in his soul to
sin, nor to differ one point from the observance
of God's commandments. Be, my son, very
charitable and an almsgiver; have about thee
honest and virtuous company; take counsel of
persons well-intentioned and virtuous; exercise
thyself in the acts of a Christian gentleman as
thy ancestors have done; govern thy vassals with
the love of a father and amorous lord; take compassion of the poor, favour the good, repress the
wicked and do justice with equality; procuring
to root out of thy estate public sins and offences
of our Lord, Whom I humbly beseech, by the
merits of His most holy Passion and of His
most holy Mother our Blessed Lady, and St.
Francis and St. Dominic, that He bless thee, and
with His blessing give thee His Divine grace and
those excellent favours which He accustometh to
give to His elect; that I, thy grandmother, and
in love more than any, as much as I can, in the
Name of the most holy Trinity, do bless thee

within and without; and conformable to this His holy blessing do again beseech Him that He obtain for thee and thy successors that which may be to the glory of the same God and good of thy soul and body, and goods and vassals. Amen. I pray thee that thou have me in thy memory, to command to say Masses for my soul, and for the souls of the duke thy father, and of the duke my lord, thy grandfather, who are in rest."

When the testament was read, signed and ratified by the justice and by the duke, order was presently taken that night to accomplish with the soonest expedition, what the testament commanded; which was principally to say Masses for her soul. For she had ordained, as soon as might be after her departure, a hundred Masses should be said in the privileged altars of the town of Madrid; and there also ordered to be sung twenty-four Masses of Requiem. In the state of Feria she had ordained to be said three thousand Masses, besides the sung Masses for nine days together, after her burial; good allowance given for all these Masses. She had bequeathed very liberally to the poor of Madrid, and to the poor monasteries there, to pray for her soul. She gave two hundred ducats to the poor of the town of *Zaphra*, and a very charitable benevolence to the monasteries there; ordering that twelve poor men should be thoroughly clothed to accompany her body at the burial, and to each of them twelve reals in money. Also she remembered with good alms our English Carthusians. No man-servant of hers but had mourning, a hat, a cassock and coat of good cloth; and the women theirs as was fit; and every one some good remembrance according to their quality and merit.

The next morning her body was put into the coffin, wrapped in lead, because it was to be carried to *Zaphra* to the monastery of Sta. Clara, there to be put in the vault under the high choir, among the other coffins of the lords of that house. She willed in her testament to be laid by the duke her husband; saying that loving together so well in life, it was meet their bodies should not be parted in death. *Zaphra* is some two-hundred English miles from Madrid, where she died. That night before she was chested, divers came to see the sweetness and fairness of that face, kissing her hands upon their knees, imagining she was in place to pray for them.

The coffin was set up high in the greater room
of the house, set round with torches and wax
lights, above and beneath, covered with a hearse-
cloth of new black velvet, which the young
duchess sent; so large, as the tomb standing
higher than a man's head, it lay spread on both
the ends and sides upon the ground. In the
same room were set up two altars, where continually from six o'clock to twelve, Masses were
said and Responsories by divers Religious. And
in the afternoon many came and prayed at the
hearse.

The day following, at three o'clock in the
morning, the body was put in a coach to be
carried to Zaphra, attended by her own servants
and twelve of the duke's (whereof his secretary
was one), her chaplain and an Augustine Friar;
for she had expressly commanded by her will to
be carried with the least pomp and the most
secret. This journey, which was nine days in
travel, (for we entered in Zaphra on the second of
February) was with the fairest weather, and as
pleasant a voyage as could be wished, although
we passed the great high mountains that part
Castille from Estramadura, (where ordinarily is
tempest and bitter storms in the winter; for in

our return we had sharp cold winds, hail and
snow) and being in the end of the month of
January, which is not a season so settled for fair
and warm .weather. And withal such a conformity and good agreement in all the company,
(albeit there were pages, under-servants and
hired fellows that served the coaches and mules,
which usually are not the most orderly), as every-
one did his duty; no murmuring, no grudging,
no complaining, nor the least disgust in the
world. Which I really have reason to attribute
to the body of our good duchess that we carried.
For divers times the same winter before she died,
in November and December, the weather being
very cold, rainy and tempestuous, she did say to
me and others: "If I should die now, what
trouble should I give my servants to carry my
body?" But then did we reply: "Fear not; she
that gave not trouble in life, will not give it in
death;" which was, as I may say, miraculously
fulfilled. And when we drew near to our journey's
end, entering into the precincts of the town of
Zaphra, it began to rain so as the whole town
cried: "The blessing of God is come;" for they
wanted rain exceedingly and had prayed long for
it; and that night they had enough, so that all

which were on horseback were thoroughly wet, and we that were in coaches were not wholly dry.

Upon Candlemas day, between five and six o'clock in the evening, we entered into *Zaphra*. Out of the town, the magistrates, gentlemen and chiefest inhabitants did meet the body with torchlight, and so accompanied it to the church of Sta. Marina, which church our duchess had built, and where lay buried the body of her cousin, Mrs. Margaret Harrington, the Lord Harrington's sister; where was erected a goodly monument in the middle of the church to place the body upon. The nuns did sing Vespers and a nocturn *de Defunctis*; which done, all the company were disposed to their lodgings in several principal men's houses, who entertained us extraordinary well.

The next morning the magistrates and we that brought the body met together at the Contador's house, who governed the estate, and with him as chief mourner went to the church, where was sung a solemn Mass and a sermon preached by a Franciscan Friar, much in praise of our duchess. In the afternoon the body was to be carried to Sta. Clara, where it was to be interred, which was done in this solemn manner. Most of the religious of all Orders in the whole estate

were present with their crosses. The Priests of
the town in their surplices and copes; the Dean
of the High Church doing the Office, having a
very rich cope of black velvet richly embroidered
with gold and the dalmatics of the deacon and
the sub-deacon answerable. These the duke her
son had caused to be made in Sicily, with the
antependiums and furniture for six altars; for so
many are in the Church of Sta. Clara; and they
are the fairest and richest ornaments to be used
pro defunctis that I have seen in Spain, or else-
where; and the first time that they were used, it
was for the duke that caused them to be made.
And albeit the way was not long between the two
monasteries, yet they made three stations, singing
a Responsory, with a prayer and incensing, certain low pillars being set, covered with black
cloth to set the body upon.

Being entered into Sta. Clara, the body was
placed on a stately high monument in the high
choir; and the nuns sung vespers and the noc-
turns of requiem. The same night, shewing to
the Abbess of Sta. Clara, who then was Donna
Maria de Mendoça, a niece of the duke of
Infantadgo, what was to be performed by the
testament of the duchess, whose will was that

her body should be there interred with the bodies
of the dukes, her husband and son; and that the
abbess, before a public notary, should accept the
conditions for accomplishing the anniversaries
and other rites ordered by the testament. The
abbess and other of the nuns answered, they
would first see whether the body were there.
For, say they, we see a coffin, but we must see
that the body is in it. Which whether it was
necessary to open the coffin being so locked, and
the body in lead, and the long time that it had
rested there would be troublesome; or that the
abbess suspected the body might be taken out, it
was questioned. For the abbess of Sta. Marina
told me that she with her religious had a purpose
that the night that the body rested in their
church to have stolen it out and to have stuffed
the coffin with some other matter, alleging that
it was proper to them, and that her body, who
was the foundress, should remain in her own
church, and it was against reason they should be
deprived of so holy a treasure so due to them. I
answered that we had the key of the coffin; and
the lock broken, it would have been perceived;
and withal it had broken her last will and desire
and would have procured much scandal and

debate; nor could I permit it, being one of the executors. "The lock seen, and the consideration thereof did only stay us, said she."

There served no reply to the abbess of Sta. Clara but she would see the body; nor would she sign nor agree to anything before she saw it, although it was fast locked and no breech at all to be seen in the coffin which, upon the boards, was covered close with black velvet, laced on the sides and ends, thick nailed with gilded nails, and double hinges fast nailed at all the corners gilded. So, to give contentment to their curiosity, the coffin was opened and the face seen, which was twelve days after her death, still remaining fair, so seemly and sweet and with so lively colours, as if she had been living; her hands tender, flexible and white, as they were while she lived. And out of her nostrils dropped a little blood, so fair, fresh and red, as if it had been from a lamb; which a priest standing there took in his handkerchief, although her body had not been opened, (for she did precisely command in her testament, charging her executors that no person should touch nor come near her body until her women had shrouded it up,) nor been dressed with spices, balms nor other drugs; so as all that saw it stood admired and might say: "*Laudabilis Deus in sanctis suis.*"

The next morning, being Saturday the 4th of February, the exequies of her funeral were to be solemnized, which continued from six o'clock in the morning to four in the evening. For first the Recollects of St. Francis's Order did sing their Nocturn and Mass so solemn as their Order may permit, with a Responsory after, sprinkling holy water and incensing about the monument. After them the Dominicans did the same also, more solemnly. After them the Franciscans did the like, the Superior still singing the Mass. Then next, the priests of the great church, the dean doing the office; the Nocturn sung and Mass celebrated most solemnly; and at the end of Mass they sung *Alternis vicibus,* five responsories, five times sprinkled, and five times incensed, about the monument. After them the nuns of the same church began their office, and after they had sung their nocturn, High Mass was celebrated; after the gospel whereof had been sung, was preached a sermon by the Prior of the Dominicans. His theme was out of the 114th Psalm, "Convertere anima mea in requiem tuam, quia Dominus beneficit tibi. Quia eripuit animam meam de morte, oculos meos a lacrymis, pedes meos a lapsu. Placebo Domino in regione vivorum;" which he applied very learnedly and divinely to the person, life and death of our duchess.

After this office was done, as the former had been, they took down the coffin to be carried down into the cave, where many other bodies lay in chests that were of the blood and descendants of the house of Feria. I was one who assisted to bear her body into that vault, which gave no offence, but with as good a savour as might be wished, was there deposed, "*ut in resurrectionis gloria inter sanctos et electos resuscitata respiret.*" Nine days after we stayed there, assisting daily at the sung Mass, which was in the church of Sta. Clara; so commanded by her Grace's will, and the ninth day the solemnity was more than ordinary.

The house of our Duchess, as she had ordered by will, remained two months, every servant there having their allowance as when she lived, to have that time to provide themselves. Presently upon our return, all legacies were paid; and before the two months were expired, all dues for Masses and other alms were discharged, and the annuities bequeathed so settled as all future questions were prevented that might hinder the due payment.

I should describe here the outward habit and constitution of the body and stature of the Duchess, which is in the history distinctly noted as she grew in years; and when I came to her service in the year 1603, in the first year of King James, she was in the sixty-sixth year of her age; which together with the heats of Spain, was much extenuated, beginning a little to stoop. She was somewhat higher than ordinary; of a comely person, a lively aspect, a gracious countenance, very clear-skinned, quick in senses; for she had her sight and hearing to her last hour. Until she broke her arm, she was perfect in all parts; her person venerable and with majesty; all showed a nobility and did win a reverent respect from all. I have not seen of her age a more fair, comely and respectful personage; which was perfected with modest comportment, deep judgment, graceful humility and true piety. Of her may be notably and really spoken those praises which are expressed in Holy Scripture of a Good Woman.

INDEX.

BOOKS FOR MEDITATION AND RETREAT.

———

1. THE CHRISTIAN REFORMED IN MIND AND MANNERS. By Father Benedict Rogacci, S.J. 7s. 6d.

2. PIOUS AFFECTIONS TOWARDS GOD AND THE SAINTS. (Meditations for every day in the Year.) By Father Nicolas Lancicius, S.J. One Vol. 7s. 6d.

3. THE LIFE AND TEACHING OF JESUS CHRIST. Arranged in Meditations for every day in the year. By Father Nicolas Avancino, S.J. Two Vols. 10s. 6d.

———

BIOGRAPHIES.

———

LIFE AND LETTERS OF ST. FRANCIS XAVIER. By the Rev. H. J. Coleridge. Two Vols. 15s. A cheaper edition in one Vol. 9s.

LIFE AND LETTERS OF ST. TERESA. By the same. Vols. I. and II. 15s. (Vol. III. in preparation.)

CHRONICLE OF ST. ANTONY OF PADUA. 3s. 6d.

STORY OF ST. STANISLAUS KOSTKA. 3s. 6d.

LIFE OF THE BLESSED JOHN BERCHMANS. By Father Goldie. 6s.

———

LONDON: BURNS AND OATES.

BIOGRAPHIES—(*Continued*).

LIFE OF CHRISTOPHER COLUMBUS. By Rev. A. Knight. 5s.

LIFE OF THE VEN. CLAUDE DE LA COLOMBIERE. 5s.

ENGLISH CARMELITE LIVES:

   1. LIFE OF MOTHER CATHARINE BURTON. New Edition. 6s.

   2. LIFE OF MOTHER MARGARET MOSTYN. New Edition 6s.

A GRACIOUS LIFE. (Mdme. Acarie) By E. Bowles. 6s.

LIFE OF ST. THOMAS OF HEREFORD. 6s.

DURING THE PERSECUTION. Autobiography of Father John Gerard, S.J. From the original Latin, by the Rev. G. R. Kingdon, S.J. 5s.

GASTON DE SEGUR. Condensed from the French Memoir by the Marquis de Segur. 3s. 6d.

LIFE OF LADY FALKLAND. By Lady G. Fullerton. 5s.

LIFE OF MOTHER MARY TERESA BALL. By Rev. H. J. Coleridge (with portrait). 7s. 6d.

LIFE OF MARY WARD. By M. C. E. Chambers, of the Institute of the Blessed Virgin. Edited by the Rev. H. J. Coleridge, S. J. 2 Vols, each 7s. 6d.

ST. MARY'S CONVENT, YORK. (History of the Convent). 7s. 6d.

LIFE OF JANE DORMER, DUCHESS OF FERIA. Immediately.

LONDON: BURNS AND OATES.

WORKS ON THE LIFE OF OUR LORD.

BY THE

REV. H. J. COLERIDGE.

———

1. THE LIFE OF OUR LIFE. Two Vols. 15s.

2. THE WORKS AND WORDS OF OUR SAVIOUR. One Vol. 7s. 6d.

3. THE STORY OF THE GOSPELS. One Vol. 7s. 6d.

THE HOLY INFANCY. Three Volumes. 7s. 6d. each. Together 20s.

    1. THE PREPARATION OF THE INCARNATION.

    2. THE NINE MONTHS. Our Lord's Life in the Womb.

    3. THE THIRTY YEARS. The Infancy and Hidden Life of Our Lord.

THE PUBLIC LIFE OF OUR LORD. Ten Volumes are now published:

    1. THE MINISTRY OF ST. JOHN BAPTIST.

    2. THE PREACHING OF THE BEATITUDES (First Part of the Sermon on the Mount.)

    3. THE SERMON ON THE MOUNT (Second Part).

    4. THE SERMON ON THE MOUNT (Third Part).

    5. THE TRAINING OF THE APOSTLES (Part I.)

    6. THE TRAINING OF THE APOSTLES (Part II.)

    7. THE TRAINING OF THE APOSTLES (Part III.).

    8. THE TRAINING OF THE APOSTLES (Part IV.)

———

LONDON: BURNS AND OATES.

WORKS ON THE LIFE OF OUR ⏐LORD— (*Continued*).

9. THE PREACHING OF THE CROSS (Part I.).
10. THE PREACHING OF THE CROSS. (Part II.). (Immediately.)
6s. 6d. each Volume.

By the same.

THE RETURN OF THE KING. Discourses on the Latter Days. 7s. 6d.

THE BAPTISM OF THE KING. Considerations on the Sacred Passion. 7s. 6d.

THE PRISONERS OF THE KING. Thoughts on the Catholic Doctrine of Purgatory. New Edition 3s. 6d.

WORKS ON OUR BLESSED LADY.

1. THE MOTHER OF THE KING. Mary during the Life of our Lord. 7s. 6d.
2. THE MOTHER OF THE CHURCH. Mary during the First Apostolic Age.

(Third Volume in Preparation.)

Edited by the same.

THE HISTORY OF THE SACRED PASSION. By Father Louis de la Palma. 7s. 6d. A cheap Edition, 5s.

THE HOURS OF THE PASSION. From the Latin of Lindolph the Saxon. 7s. 6d.

THE SEVEN WORDS ON THE CROSS. By Cardinal Bellarmine. 5s.

LONDON: BURNS AND OATES.

104